Lewis Morley

Introduction by Terence Pepper

Scandalous Bodies by David Mellor

National Portrait Gallery Publications

Lewis Morley
photographer of the sixties

Published for the exhibition held from 15 September 1989 to 7 January 1990
at the National Portrait Gallery, London

Exhibition organizers: Terence Pepper and Robin Gibson
Exhibition designer: Caroline Brown

Published by National Portrait Gallery Publications, National Portrait Gallery,
St Martin's Place, London WC2H 0HE, England, 1989

British Library Cataloguing in Publication Data
Morley, Lewis
Lewis Morley: photographer of the sixties. Introduction by Terence Pepper
1. English, photography. Morley, Lewis – catalogues, indexes
1. Title II. National Portrait Gallery. Great Britain
779'.09'4

ISBN 1 85514 003 9

Catalogue edited by Gillian Forrester. Designed by Richard Smith & Cara Gallardo, Area
Typesetting by Ampersand Typesetting (London) Limited. Printed by BAS Printers Limited

Front cover: Christine Keeler, 1963 (detail) (no. 89)
Back cover: John Betjeman (no. 88)

Photographic acknowledgements
All photographs are by Lewis Morley. The exhibition organizers would like to thank the following for giving permission to reproduce copyright items: by courtesy of *Tatler* (fig. 5); by courtesy of *Woman's Own* (fig. 11)

Thanks to Shura Shihwarg, Willy Donaldson and Patricia Morley who made this possible – Lewis Morley

contents

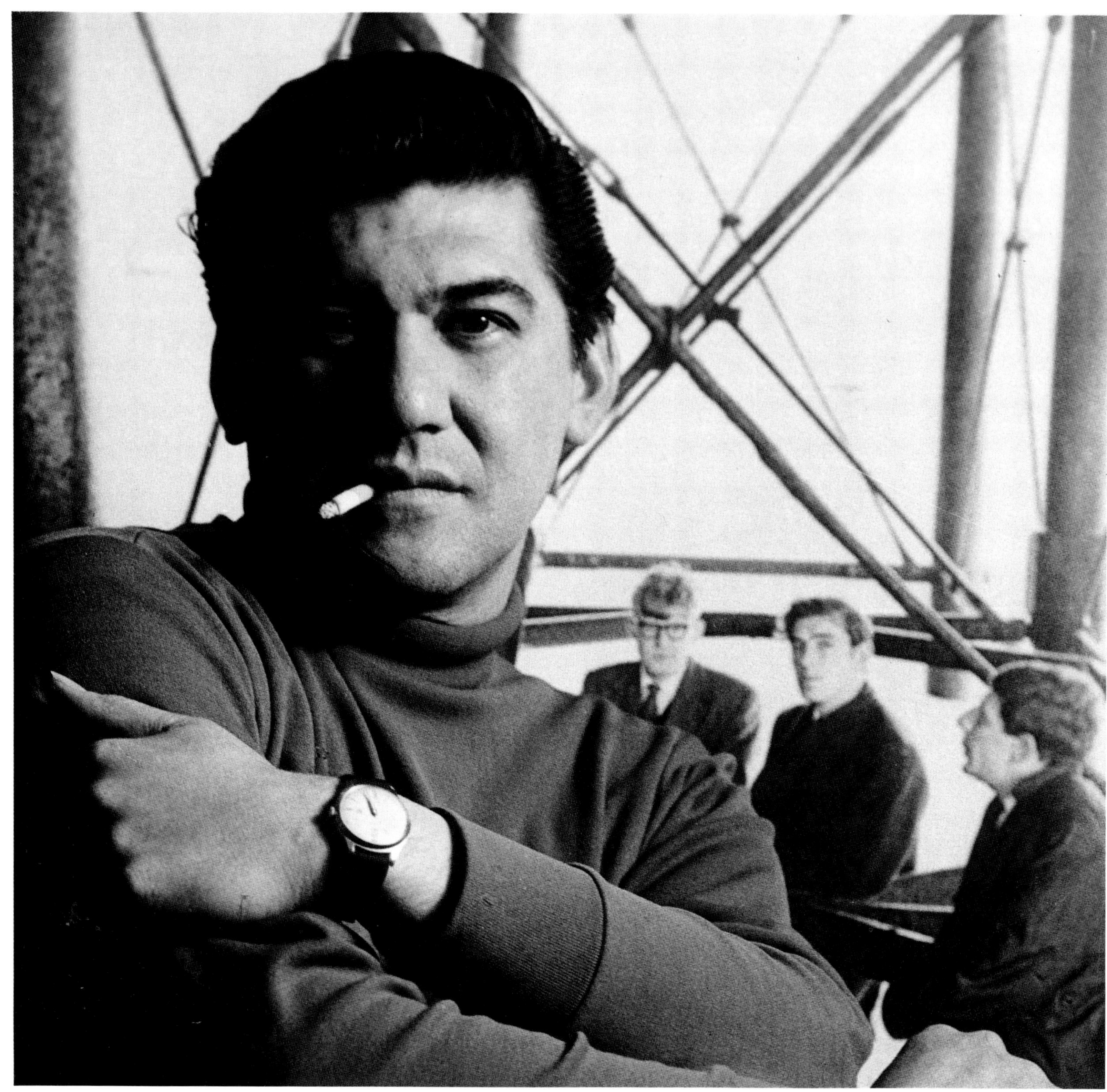

Self-portrait, 1961

It is a distinction attained by few photographers to have produced the definitive images of not only one but two key figures in recent social and cultural history. Neither Christine Keeler nor Joe Orton made Lewis Morley's name however, and he, like they, disappeared for a time from sight to await resurrection in the nostalgia-hungry eighties. Unlike other photographers of his generation who managed to hold their ground, Morley was no showman and was working at a time when not only were photographers' names seldom credited but photography was still a craft, unsanctified by the exhibitions in art galleries and museums which are now a commonplace.

Morley has generously given prints to the Collection over the past few years and it has been greatly encouraging to find that the rest of the considerable output of his London period was as fresh and original as the few images we knew. It is the pleasant task of the National Portrait Gallery to ensure that Morley's name becomes, perhaps, nearly as well known as the subjects of his photographs and that he takes his rightful place alongside the other great image-makers of the period.

We owe a considerable debt to the photographer for his generosity and patience in supplying prints and information for the exhibition and catalogue, and to Kodak Australasia in the person of Mark Lee for his enthusiastic support for the project from its inception and for supplying Kodak paper for all the exhibition prints. Thanks must also go to Terry Hamaton, Joan Wyndham, Shura Shihwarg, Rhianon Finamore of the Theatre Museum, Tony Rushton of *Private Eye*, the John Frost Historical Newspaper Service, and not least to David Mellor for his stimulating essay.

Robin Gibson
Terence Pepper

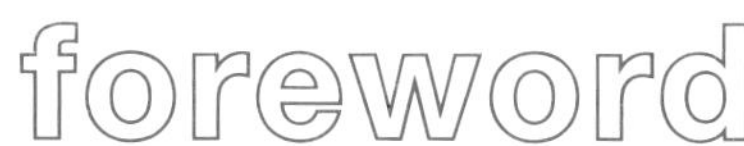

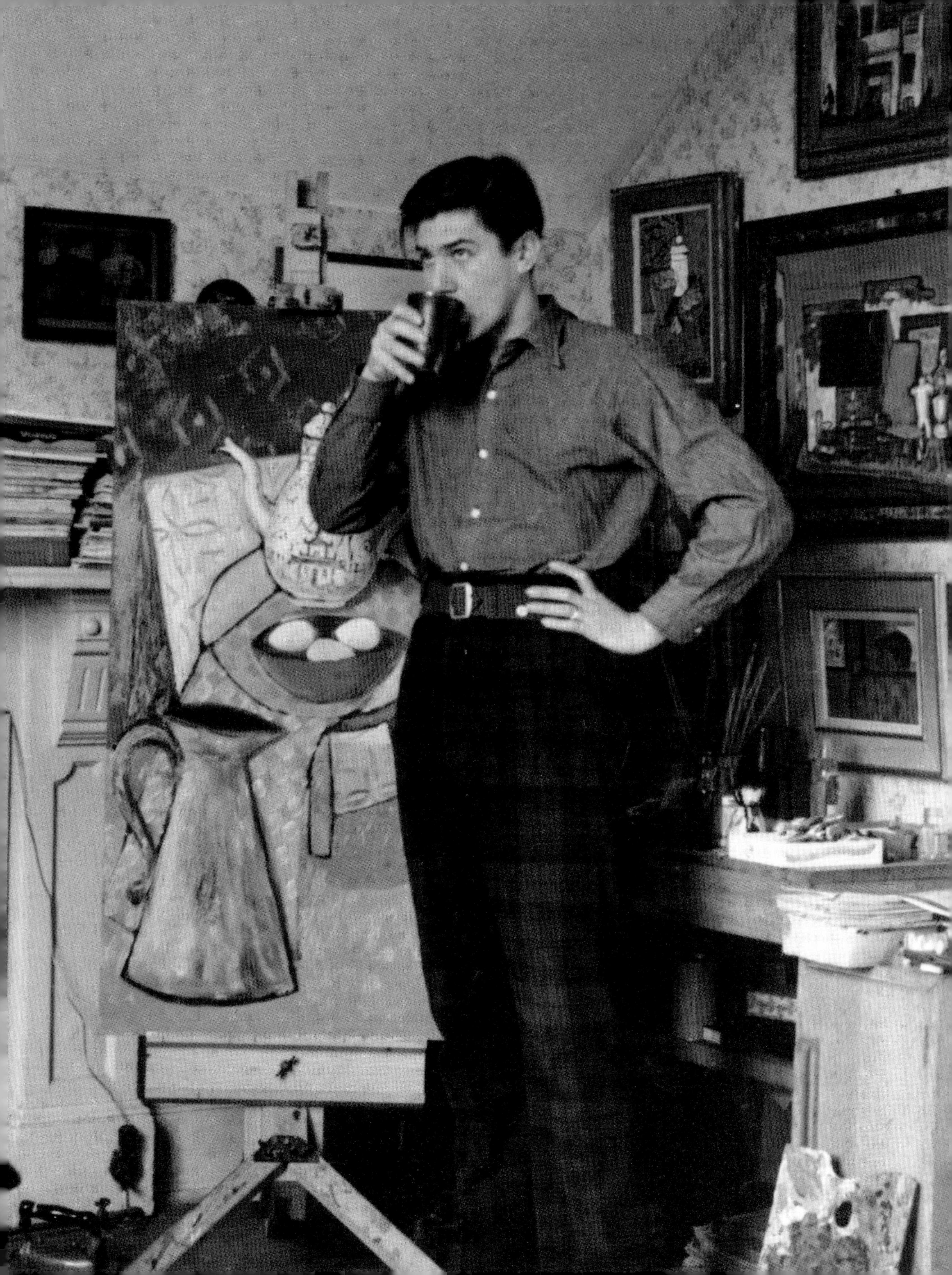

The 1960s in Britain was a time of major social, cultural and political upheaval. Class barriers began to crumble as new role models emerged from newly socially acceptable professions. Clothes designers, fashion models, pop stars, hairdressers and even photographers were elevated into the new élite. Social realism pervaded the cinema and theatre, and the 'satire boom' in print, on the stage and on television epitomized the changing attitudes to the old order of authority and tradition. The newly elected Labour government of 1964 began a programme of social legislation which seemed to usher in a new permissive society. London became the epicentre of the swinging sixties. Lewis Morley worked throughout this period and chronicled the new idols of society in a style which captured the buoyant spirit of the times. Like David Bailey, the most famous of the photographers of the sixties, Lewis Morley first became interested in photography while serving in the RAF (1946-9) although his first ambition was to be a painter.

Lewis Frederick Morley was born in Hong Kong on 16 June 1925. He was half-Chinese on his mother's side. His father was Chief Pharmacist to the Colony. During the Second World War Morley was interned with his family in the Stanley Civilian Camp by the occupying Japanese forces. Watercolours he made there of the Japanese camp guards as a teenager later won him a place at Twickenham College of Art (1949-52) where he studied after leaving the RAF. He completed a graphic design course and spent a year as a commercial artist with the Colman, Prentis and Varley advertising agency. Finding this unfulfilling, he left after a year when he was offered studio space in Paris. He attended life drawing classes at the Académie La Grande Chaumière in the company of many expatriot American GIs, and lived off the sale of his paintings.

In 1954 he returned to London to marry Patricia Clifford, a commercial illustrator. He secured a job at night as a telephone operator which allowed him to paint during the day. He also bought his first Leica and became more involved in photography. The birth of his son Lewis Morley Jnr. in 1957 coincided with the first publication of his work in a six-page portfolio in *Photography.* Introduced with a text by Norman Hall, the legendary picture editor, Morley was announced as the latest 'Young Britain' discovery. The text told of Morley's decision to forsake the paint-brush for the camera and was prefaced with a pre-marriage self-portrait (1954) of the artist surrounded by his Bernard Buffetesque paintings in a crowded bed-sitting room (fig. 1).

Morley's first published photographs show the pervasive influence of the greatest of all photo-journalists, Henri Cartier-Bresson. In *Bride in the Rain* (fig. 2), Morley captures Cartier-Bresson's 'decisive moment' as his subject escapes from the rain near Hammersmith Broadway, while in *Trooping The Colour* (fig. 3), Morley, like Cartier-Bresson in his famous study taken for George V's Coronation of onlookers in Trafalgar Square, points his camera at telling faces corralled behind a makeshift crowd barrier. Through a friend in the RAF, John Sloss, who had also been interned in Hong Kong, Morley was introduced to the writer Joan Wyndham (no. 8) and her husband Shura Shihwarg, who managed a small press agency in Fleet Street. Shihwarg helped Morley to secure several magazine assignments at the start of his career, through his contacts, and one of the most important of these was for *Tatler*, to which Morley became a regular contributor from 1958 onwards. Morley's early photo-journalistic study of Geoffrey Fisher, Archbishop of Canterbury (fig. 4) embraces the best elements of a 1930s candid portrait by Eric Saloman. Other portrait commissions for *Tatler* included studies of the brilliant American designer, Raymond Loewy (no. 11) and Somerset Maugham, both taken whilst on assignment for the magazine in the South of France, and Salvador Dali, Osbert Sitwell and newly married Peter Hall and Leslie Caron in London (no. 17).

1 **Self-portrait**, 1954 (no. 2)

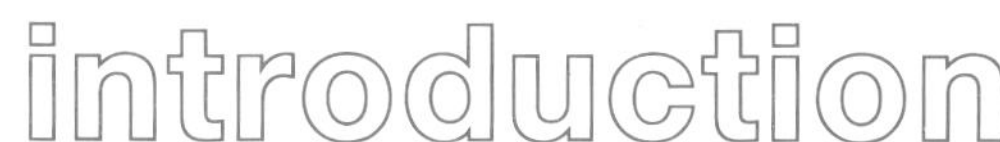

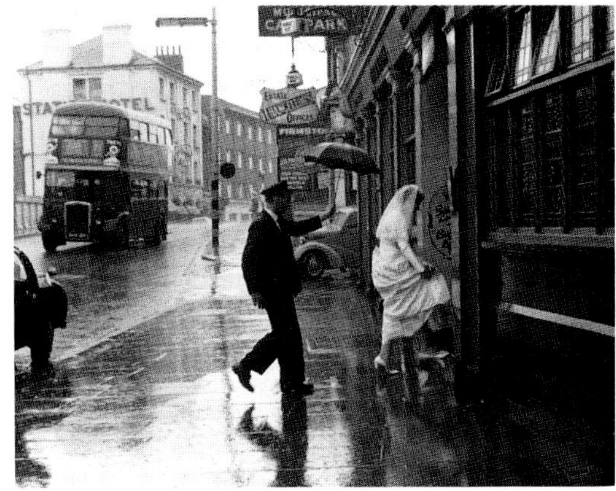
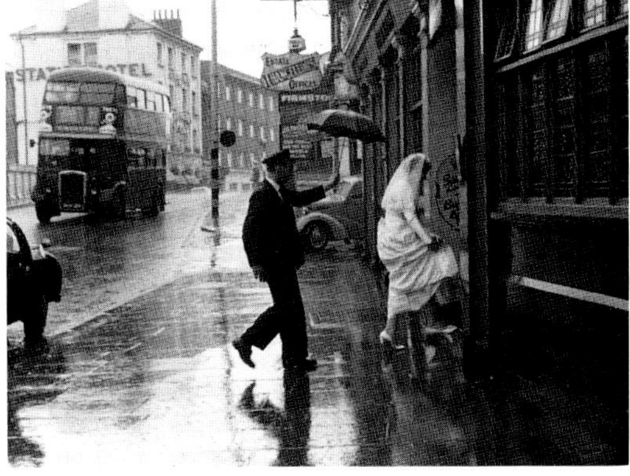

2 **Bride in the Rain**, 1957 (no. 3)

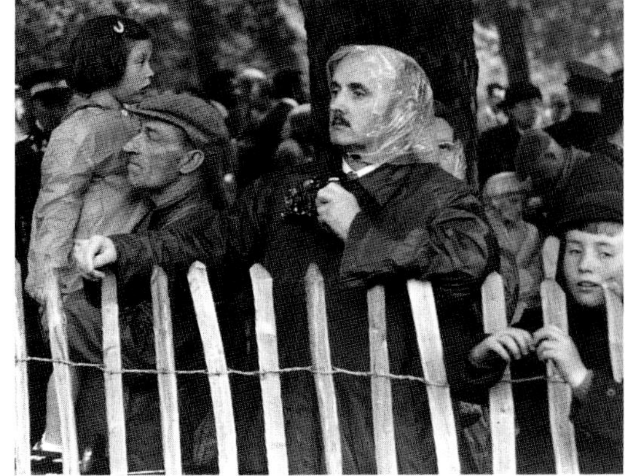

3 **Watching the Trooping of the Colour**, 1957 (no. 4)

For a feature in *Tatler* entitled *The Day of the Swot at Cambridge* (13 April 1960), Morley teamed up for the first time with the writer William Donaldson, who was also a director of Panaramic Studios in Marshall Street, Soho. Morley moved in to share the space and facilities and soon became the sole photographer in charge – the studio name becoming Lewis Morley Studios. Assignments for *Tatler* continued into the mid-1960s and included a portfolio on the new red-brick University of Sussex for the 15 July 1964 issue with a colour cover of the ubiquitous Jay twins, the trend-setting, Courrèges-booted daughters of the Labour cabinet minister, Douglas Jay (fig. 5).

Unlike his contemporaries who specialized in specific fields such as reportage, fashion and portraiture, Morley worked across a very broad range of subjects. As a fashion photographer he first worked in 1961 for *Go!* (edited by John Anstey with Jocelyn Stevens as editor-in-chief, and Mark Boxer as art director). An early assignment was a fashion session at a race meeting; this also happened to be Jean Shrimpton's first modelling job (no. 37). For a feature shot in Paris later that year, he worked with the young film actress, Susannah York, paired with the model (now photographer) David Hamilton. Hamilton stepped in when York's husband Mike Wells was unavailable for the shoot, but Morley captured the couple in a café in the Paris flea market, during a production break (no. 36).

From 1962 onwards, Morley worked regularly for the National Magazine Company's monthly *She* magazine. Its regular star columnists included Nancy Spain (no. 34) and Kenneth Horne. Morley's fashion work for them often featured celebrities such as Bobby Moore, Jimmy Tarbuck and Willie Rushton. Dave Clark (no. 47) and Billy J. Kramer with Heinz (no. 44), appeared in clothes designed by John Stephen, one of the sixties' most prominent designers. One of Morley's most fascinating insights into sixties fashion is his behind-the-scenes shot of stylists arranging a hapless model in impractical chain-mail costume (fig. 9); but it is the unfashionably rumpled clothes, the tinted, wire-framed glasses, and the hairstyles inspired by the musical 'Hair', of the stylist and assistants which are more telling hallmarks of the time than the fantastical outfit commissioned by the magazine.

Morley's early study of Twiggy, for a street-fashion feature for Theo Goldrey in *London Life*, like his earlier portrait of Jean Shrimpton, captures an historic moment of sixties fashion (no. 38). Taken shortly after her meeting with her friend and manager Justin de Villeneuve, it shows the young Twiggy, an ex-hairdresser's assistant, caught with an anonymous brown paper parcel and wearing a second-hand fur coat bought for £5 in the Portobello Road. It was taken several months before Twiggy became an overnight sensation, when Barry Lategan's photograph announced her in *The Daily Express* as the 'Face of 1966'. Equally guileless, nostalgic and evocative of youthful innocence is Morley's portrait of Charlotte Rampling lying on her candlewick bedspread in her London flat, flanked by her favourite teddy bear and simple transistor radio, the essential youth accessory of the 1960s (no. 39). Both studies capture the unsophisticated allure of two of the most influential style-setters of the decade.

Morley made portraits of couples a particular speciality. He recorded John Cleese and Connie Booth (no. 59) in 1968, just after their marriage, in a double profile emphasizing their close relationship, and using a variation of this silhouette pose, photographed Felicity Kendal and Drewe Henley at the time of their engagement (no. 58). Morley reserved his most imaginative portraits for his closest friends. In an elaborate composition to pay homage to Benvenuto Cellini's salt-cellar, he photographed his friend Anthony Fry, the painter, with his girl friend and child, Wild, in a floral-tiled bathroom full of telling period detail (fig. 6). Kenny Everett, at the time a pirate-radio disc jockey for Radio Caroline, is portrayed with his wife and pets in a suitably over-charged, lace-decorated scene of mayhem that well conveys Everett's ebullient characteristics (no. 46).

As a photographer of pop groups, Morley had a mixed success, depending on the extent of the co-operation from his subjects. Commissioned by their manager, Simon Napier-Bell, Morley recorded The Yardbirds, both in stills and in early pop video form. When Jeff Beck went solo in 1967 Morley iconized him with his two crucial sixties accessories, an Afghan coat and an Afghan hound (no. 54). For the same manager he also recorded the first line-up of the very 'Mod' group The Small Faces in 1963 (no. 45).

Morley's most famous and most widely copied pop portrait is of the folk singer Donovan with his fingers upside-down cupped as spectacles over his eyes (no. 55). Donovan was signed to Pye Records in 1964, as the British answer to Bob Dylan. Both sang in folk-style with guitars, and

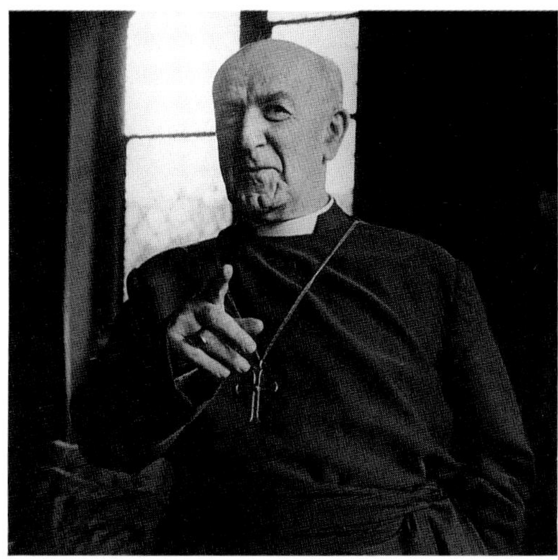

4 **Geoffrey Fisher, Archbishop of Canterbury**, 1960 (no. 13)

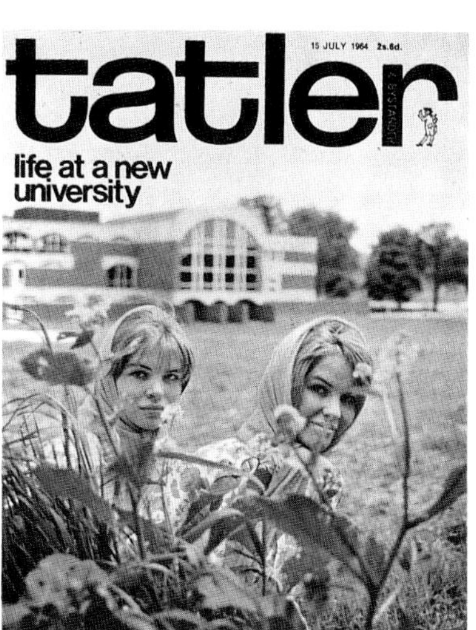

5 Cover for **Tatler**, 15 July 1964

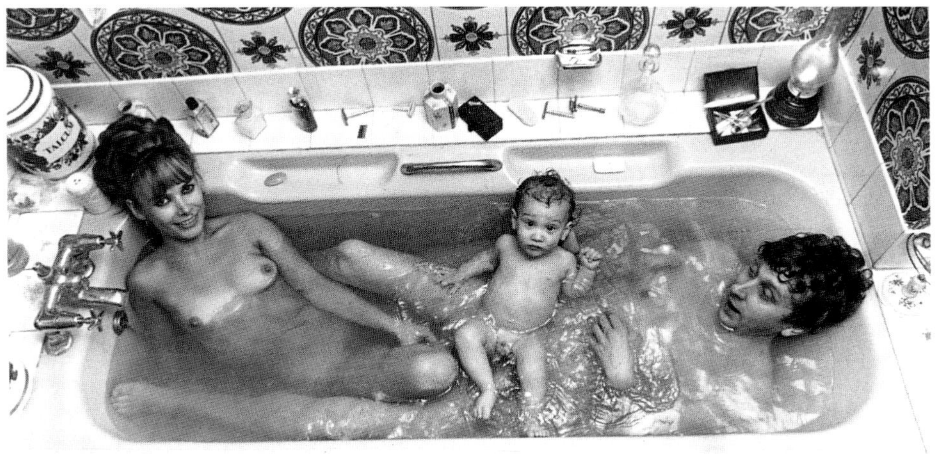

6 **Sheila Scott-James, Anthony Fry and Wild**, 1964 (no. 51)

Donovan clearly emulated the famous American in his choice of sartorial accoutrements of denim jacket and peaked cap. Donovan met Dylan during the latter's British tour in 1965 and Dylan saw the Morley portrait. When Dylan later posed for Annie Leibovitz in 1977, he adopted the Donovan pose which other, lesser, stars continue to do.

A large proportion of Morley's work throughout the sixties was devoted to theatre photography which included front-of-house pictures, programme illustrations and general publicity photographs for actors, playwrights and designers. Morley's entry into theatre photography came when the director, Lindsay Anderson, previously a documentary film-maker, invited him to take programme photographs, in addition to front-of-house pictures already taken by Tony Armstrong-Jones (later Lord Snowdon) for the 1959 Royal Court production of John Arden's *Serjeant Musgrave's Dance*. Tony Armstrong-Jones had pioneered a new type of theatre photography in the late 1950s for plays such as John Osborne's *The Entertainer* with Laurence Olivier; he produced massive grainy blow-ups of the actors' faces using only available stage lighting. These gave an immediate and journalistic impression of action and movement which suited the new 'Look Back in Anger' style of theatre. This approach was in complete contrast to the immaculately-lit, carefully-posed tableaux, at which photographers such as Angus McBean were master craftsmen. Morley's journalistic capabilities and quick eye made him ideally fitted to take this new kind of instantaneous record shot which conveyed the spirit of the drama in an urgent and telling way. For his next major play, *Billy Liar*, Lindsay Anderson commissioned Morley to take all the photographs. Morley broke with tradition and took pictures of Finney leaning against a brick wall outside the theatre in Cambridge Circus (no. 23), as well as more conventional on-stage production photographs. Morley achieved a naturalness and immediacy which suited the contemporary spirit of the play and the time, exemplified by a study which adorned a sheet music cover for the play's hit song (fig. 7). The play opened in September 1960, to enormous critical and box office success. During its long run the cast changed twice and Morley continued the pictorial documentation. In June 1961 Tom Courtenay (no. 22) took over the lead as Billy Fisher and was subsequently replaced by Trevor Bannister. Courtenay eventually appeared in the title role in the film in 1963.

Morley renewed his collaboration with William Donaldson when the latter was co-producer with Donald Albery of a new revue which opened at the Fortune Theatre in May 1961. *Beyond the Fringe* had been commissioned by John Bassett to form part of the official programme for the previous year's Edinburgh Festival. The title referred to the Festival Fringe which had seen two successful Cambridge revues in previous years. The cast of performers and writers had not worked together before. Alan Bennett and Dudley Moore came from Oxford, while Jonathan Miller and Peter Cook were from Cambridge. At the time the revue seemed subversive; it dealt with subjects such as religion, nuclear defence, capital punishment and racism, and included a parody of Harold Macmillan which broke with the convention of the times by satirizing respected public figures. Morley's front-of-house pictures also broke with tradition. Without making any specific reference to the revue sketches, as was the normal practice, he photographed the cast acting zanily on location at Brighton, at the bus terminus and on the beach, and in London, at Regent's Park Zoo (fig. 14; nos. 61-3). His photographs anticipate Richard Lester's subsequent direction of The Beatles for their first film *A Hard Day's Night* (1964), where another group of four characters is stage-managed into off-beat, snapshot situations and poses. Morley's photograph for the LP cast recording (fig. 8) includes motifs which characterize the sixties. Posed against the painted hoardings near Regent's Park the composition becomes an Op Art creation like a Bridget Riley painting. The stripes operate as an emblematic and patterned background which unites but individualizes the four differing talents. Like *Billy Liar*, *Beyond the Fringe* ran successfully for several years, and a replacement cast of Terence Brady, Joe Melia, Robin Ray and Bill Wallis took over when the original cast took the revue to New York in October 1962. The relationship Morley built up with the cast during this assignment ensured his continued role as photographer for a wide number of Peter Cook and Dudley Moore collaborations including their later *Behind the Fridge* (1972) and their book *Dagenham Papers* (1971).

Beyond the Fringe marked the start of the brief early 1960s 'satire boom' and Morley became its official photographer. In October 1961 Peter Cook took over the Club Tropicana night-club in Greek Street and with Nick Luard as partner turned it into The Establishment Club, a venue

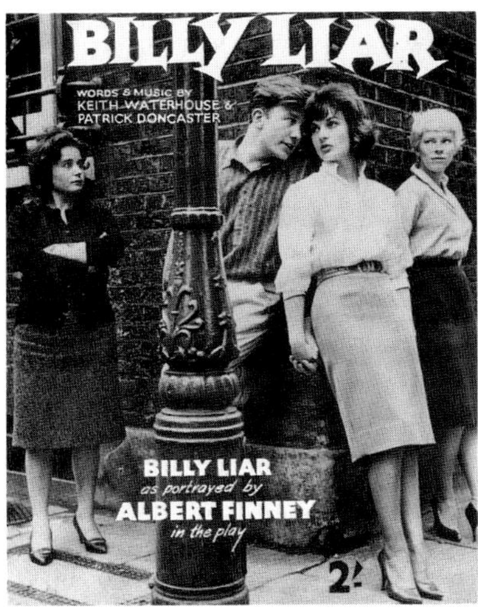

7 Sheet music cover for **Billy Liar**

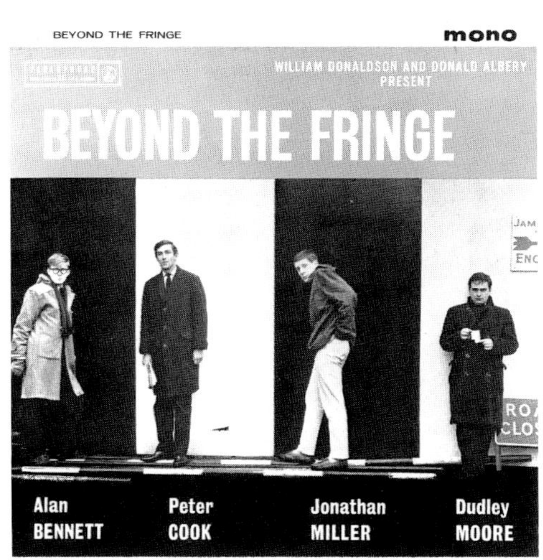

8 Cover for **Beyond the Fringe** LP, 1961

for uncensored revue and satire. Cook acquired the whole building; he sub-let the upper floors to Sean Kenny, the stage designer (no. 32) and the first floor to Lewis Morley while the Dudley Moore Trio played jazz in the basement. Morley was ideally placed to record most of the Establishment productions. At the same time Richard Ingrams, Christopher Booker and William Rushton produced the first issue of the satirical magazine *Private Eye*; Peter Cook became principal shareholder the following April, while continuing as contributor.

Morley contributed photographs to *Private Eye* throughout the sixties including 'shocking' covers and montages where, for example, Prince Philip (1967) or Alec Douglas-Home (1963) were featured using heads shot from agency photographs pasted onto photographs of Ingrams's or Rushton's body to make a satirical point (see *Scandalous Bodies*). The satire boom continued in another arena when Ned Sherrin put together for BBC Television a weekly topical satire show, *That Was The Week That Was*, better known as *TW3*, which was first broadcast in November 1962. In addition to *Private Eye* writers, the programme introduced David Frost as presenter (no. 71), and featured critics such as Bernard Levin (nos. 68, 69) and established cabaret stars including Millicent Martin (no. 70). The sketches often used stop-action stills and other pieces of photographica provided by Morley, the programme's official credited photographer.

The most memorable of all Morley's photographs taken in his studio are those of Christine Keeler and Joe Orton. Keeler, at the height of the unfolding Profumo scandal was brought to the studio to pose for publicity photographs for a planned film of her life-story, in which she was to appear, to be made by Topaz Films. Morley's now classic photograph of Keeler posed naked on a studio chair against a plain backdrop was first published uncredited in the *Sunday Mirror* of 9 June 1963, when Stephen Ward was about to be charged. Further poses accompanied Keeler's *News of the World* confessions and subsequently newspapers throughout the world disseminated the image. The Keeler portrait is one of the most famous icons of the period and it was immediately copied and adapted for a number of purposes and has been ever since. One of the studies was adapted by Gerald Scarfe for a back cover of *Private Eye* in a biting attack on the Macmillan government's inability to contain this and other scandals. In the line drawing, Macmillan's head is attached to Keeler's naked fleshed-out body, sitting in half-profile on Morley's studio chair. Soon afterwards the Pop Art painter and actress Pauline Boty (whom Morley had first photographed in 1959 for William Hickey as secretary of the Anti-Ugly League) incorporated the image in a painting entitled *Scandal '63*, which also included Profumo. More recently, Lord Snowdon has photographed Peter Boydell QC naked in the Morley chair pose, while Palace Pictures used Morley's Keeler picture extensively to promote the British release of the 1989 film *Scandal*, even though it had no direct relevance to any specific scene in the film. For the advertising poster for the US release of *Scandal*, the leading actress Joanne Whalley was photographed in colour, imitating the pose of Morley's portrait. The strength of the image and its simplicity has ensured its longevity and place in the visual history of the pin-up (see *Scandalous Bodies* for further discussion of this image). Joe Orton's portrait on the same studio chair was one of a series taken in 1965 for the American production of his play *Entertaining Mr Sloane* (Morley had photographed it for its first production at the Arts Theatre in 1964). Orton was anxious to be seen as Britain's most physically well-built playwright, in a field in which there were probably few other contestants. Morley's close-up, half-length, body-builder pose of Orton was used for the cover of John Lahr's official biography *Prick Up Your Ears* (1978) (fig. 15).

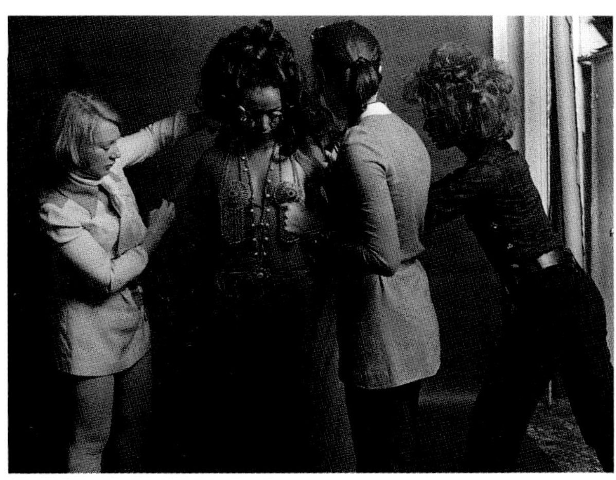

9 **Stylists prepare a model for chain-mail fashion feature**, 1969 (no. 79)

Throughout the decade Morley continued theatre photography. In the eleven years from 1959 to 1970 he photographed nearly a hundred major West End productions and established himself as one of the major talents in this specialized profession. Most of his early work was for the producer Oscar Lewenstein but from 1963 onwards he documented among others almost all Michael Codron's productions ranging from the experimental David Halliwell play of 1966, *Little Malcolm and his Struggle against the Eunuchs* (no. 77) to his blander but longer-running successes of the late 1960s such as *The Flip Side* (1967) and *There's a Girl in My Soup* (1966). One of the last plays Morley photographed was Oscar Panizza's *Council of Love* (1970), newly translated by John Bird and produced by William Donaldson. It featured Warren Mitchell as Satan (no. 76). The play was set over an Easter weekend in 1495 with scenes set in Heaven, Hell, Earth and the Vatican, and allowed for scenes of extensive orgies and nudity. The expected outcry anticipated by the play's promoters failed to materialize from a jaded public, hardened after a decade of change and 'shocks'. It was nevertheless a suitable moment for Morley to change direction. On the advice of several friends who had already moved there, Morley decided to emigrate with his family to Australia to begin a new life in Sydney. One of his last assignments was a collaboration with John Betjeman (no. 88; illustrated back cover). Morley photographed some of the worst of the new architecture in London for Betjeman's *Private Eye* column. Betjeman recommended the move away from London and wrote a poem for Morley to wish him well.

Once in Australia Morley began a new and productive career photographing mainly in colour, and specializing in interior design and personality portraiture on location, for the prestigious *Belle* magazine, in partnership with the features writer Babette Hayes. He continued working throughout the 1970s and most of the 1980s, and only retired from active photography in 1987 after a final assignment to photograph a surreal Benson and Hedges advertisement in San Francisco. Since then he has been involved in the major task of rediscovering his enormous output of the last thirty-plus years to make this exhibition possible.

Terence Pepper

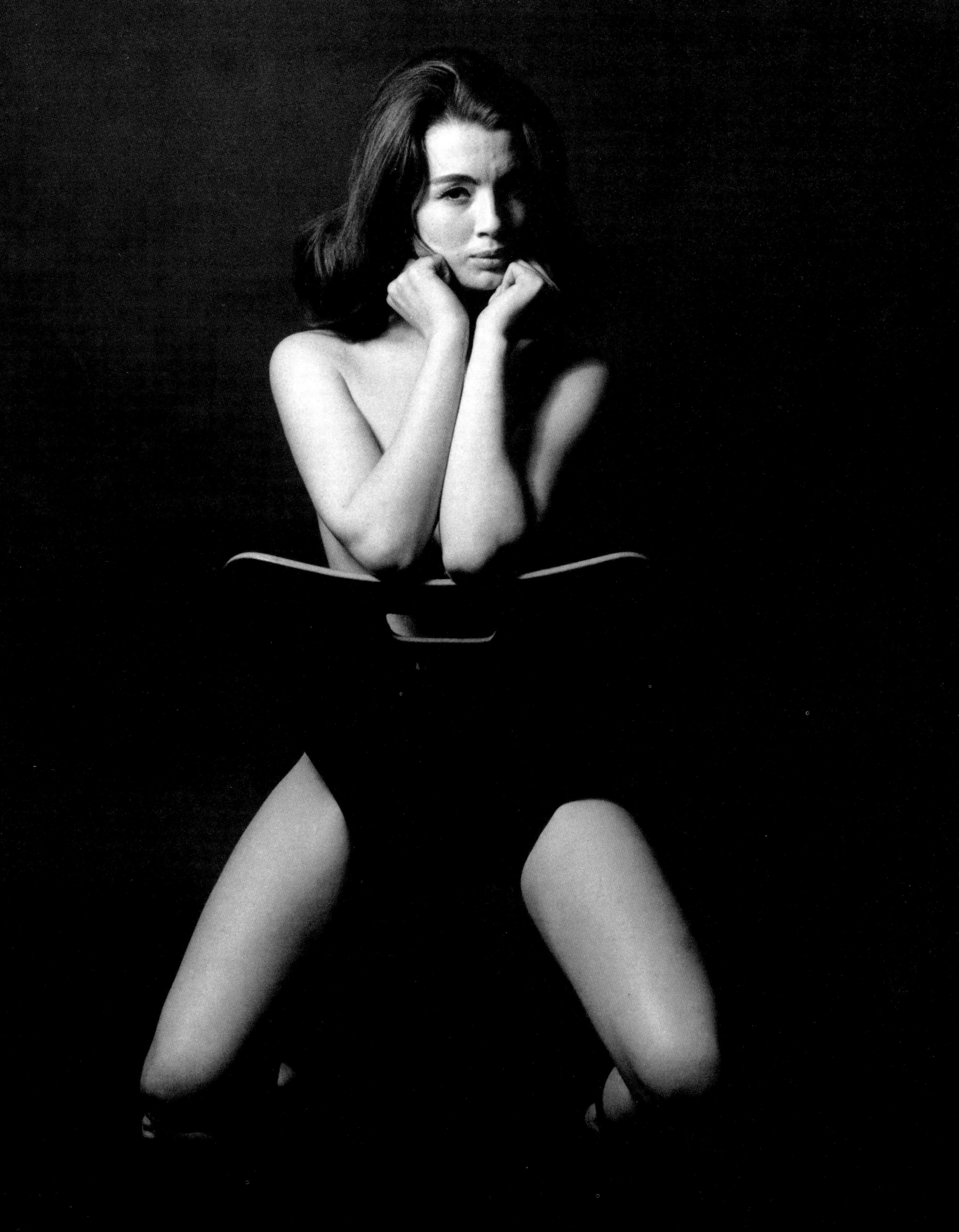

The Carnival of the Sixties

It is the bitter spring of 1963. The satirist is sneering behind a coarse, grey, 425-line television screen, his exclamatory face bulging, while a news-columnist's mouth is all agape. The pop-group manager strikes a 'switched on' pose on the Mersey dockside (fig. 11), while Christine, the Model, straddles a chair in Soho. These are bodies drawn from British pop culture who promiscuously sprawl and protrude across media representations from this moment: their bodies constitute this moment. They are, above all, Lewis Morley's scandalous bodies. Carnival as a cultural category would, perhaps, be an effective way of understanding these photographs: placing them within an imaginary network of the grotesque and a sense of the world turned upside-down. Carnival appears as the disorderly ruling metaphor in the visual imagination of the sixties; visible in the cartoons of Timothy Birdsall in *The Spectator* and *Private Eye*[1], and in the paintings of Pauline Boty, too[2]. We might imagine Morley's unstable grounding in the carnivalesque at the very beginning of his career as a photographer, on the eve of the new decade, when he made a photo-essay on a fairground.[3] Introduced in *Tatler* by a huge capital F for Fairground, a letter grotesquely composed from the faces of grimacing uneven-toothed showmen, Morley was referring to that populist style of carnivalesque photography to be found in *Lilliput* and *Picture Post* in the forties and fifties. In its stead, in the sixties, Morley forcefully instated a vision of British society spilling over in its transit across profound social dislocations.

As a strategic formulator of representations within the 'satire industry' through his work for *That Was The Week That Was* and *Private Eye*, he played upon the destabilised hierarchies of a mutating British culture during this period of political and social carnival. 'One might say that carnival celebrates temporary liberation from the prevailing truth of the established order; it marks the suspension of all hierarchical rank, privileges, norms and prohibitions', wrote the literary theorist Mikhail Bakhtin.[4] Thus the satirical moment of the early and mid-sixties was the counterpart to a perceived – yet temporary – faltering of the hegemonic structures of British culture.

Christine's Domain

Naked, she ambivalently sits astride two categories of the nude, *nuditas virtualis* (vulnerability and innocence) and *nuditas criminalis* (lasciviousness and vain exhibition). The media saturnalia of the summer of 1963, fascinated with its representation of her, her texts and her 'confessions', became a *charivari*[5] which was ultimately directed against her. She was desired *and* reviled at the same time: – 'Carnival often violently abuses and demonises … women … Its failure to do away with the official dominant culture, [is] its licensed complicity'.[6] When Pauline Boty came to paint her picture of the Profumo Affair, *Scandal '63* (1963), for an anonymous patron, she was photographed by Morley holding the painting (no. 48). It is a measure of the power of Morley's portrait of Christine that, when Boty's picture was exhibited at the Grabowski Gallery a month or two later she had repainted it, giving much of the canvas over to an appropriation of his photograph of Christine, juxtaposed below other press images of her lovers. 'I've tried to give them a photographic harshness …', Boty wrote.[7] High contrast, dark and 'harsh'; Morley's photograph became a point of citation for Boty and others, ringed by plagiarism, parody and replication.

The Satirical Nude

In Boty's painting Christine is in the lower half of the canvas, below the photo-press version

) **Christine Keeler**, 1963

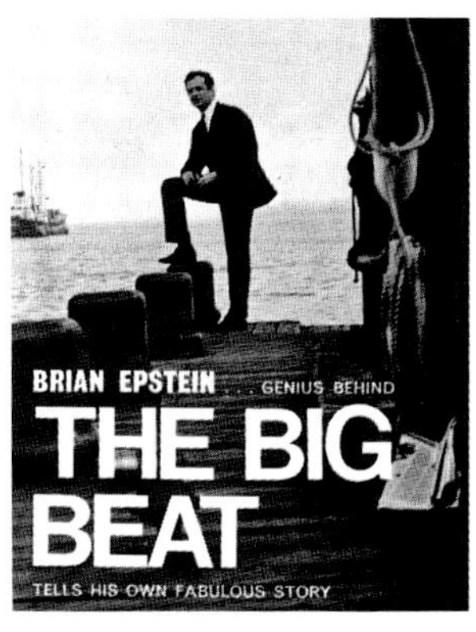

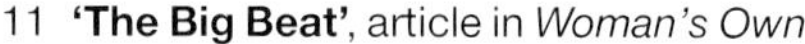
11 **'The Big Beat'**, article in *Woman's Own*

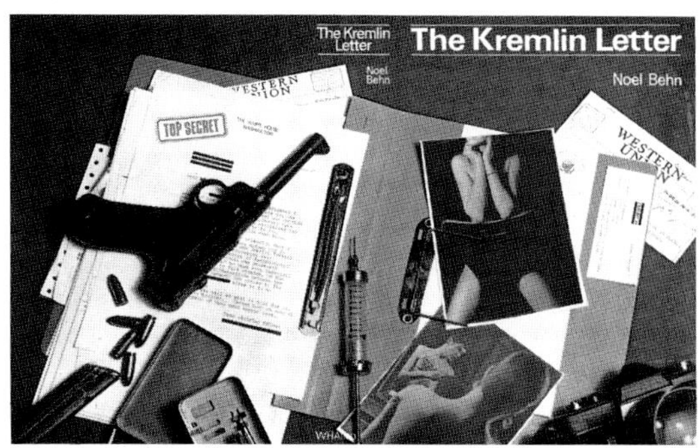

12 **The Kremlin Letter** book jacket

of Profumo, the socially 'high' who 'includes that low symbolically as the primary eroticised constituent of its own fantasy life'.[8] But Morley's type-image of Christine also had an immediate context, in his milieu inside the 'satire industry'. In the spring of 1963, his fellow *Private Eye* colleagues Barry Fantoni and William Rushton successfully submitted a painting for the Royal Academy Summer Exhibition, *Nude Reclining*. This showed 'a crudely drawn cardinal, general and judge, all in their robes of office, peering down at a book of pin-ups'[9], a satirical *topos* of socially 'high' hypocrisy gazing at the 'low', similar to Jean Genet's *The Balcony* (1957), which comprised the fantasies of a bishop, general and a judge in a brothel. (This play was premiered at the Arts Theatre in the heyday of the dissentient 'Angry' culture of London in the late fifties). But, unlike *Nude Reclining*, in Morley's portrait the naked Christine looks back, brazenly, with a steady and even gaze.

From Showman to Showgirl

A facetious quotation from 'low' genres: the pin-up or else the beckoning front-of-house photographs of the stripper or showgirl draped about the prop of the chair; these were among the contemporary connotations of the Christine portrait. It was, in addition, the convention of the time for entertainers – like Sinatra, Sammy Davis Jnr.[10], even Millicent Martin, the singer in *TW3* – to perch spotlit on spindly 'contemporary design' stools and chairs. Morley's studio chair was just such a paradigm of functional good taste; an Arne Jacobsen chair of the fifties, purchased at Heals and now the container for something transgressive, an illicit body. The adequate contemporary slang term was 'kinky'. Around her, the black space reads like the darkened stage for a performance in an 'intimate revue'; a corner of that Soho world where a striptease club might metamorphose into a satirical night-club as The Establishment did in the summer of 1961. (And, of course, it was precisely here that Morley photographed her, in his studio directly over The Establishment.)

From the chair metaphors of the body and seeing are generated; slipping up and over, a waisted template mimics her body. But no *Violon d'Ingres* this: the chair's back forms a barrier to the fascinated (male) gaze. That plywood back becomes Barthes' 'ultimate triangle ... [which] bars the way to the sexual parts like a sword of purity and definitively drives the woman back'.[11] Such a tactic Morley had used to convince Christine to pose naked: she would ultimately be hidden.[12] Through her transgressive body Christine registers the limits of this carnival of British culture in the early sixties and the Profumo affair in particular; the chair back is the cynosure, 'sensual' in itself according to Morley, but also an opaque and obvious barrier, a metaphor of repression and censorship. Yet, with the hand-hold cut into the chair back, an aperture onto her body is promised, an opening. However, the 'low' truth, like her lower bodily strata, paradoxically remains veiled while pruriently well publicized[13] in the texts and confessions of that summer.

Seeing and Spying

A few months later *Town* magazine, in its prescient survey of 'The Age of Macmillan', characterized it as 'an age of excess, [with] too many secrets in too many hands'.[14] The master trope of secrecy, of spying, was put in circulation through the disclosing gaze of the woman, the loose gaze of Vanity, first inverting then affirming and buttressing a fetishism of power. A prime example would be the first 'Bond Girl', Vesper Lynd[15], who is introduced into Fleming's text, by being discovered by James Bond as she spies out gambling secrets with binoculars, astride a chair in the pose of Christine. 'U-2 can be a spy' ran the punning caption to Morley's promotional photograph of a woman taking covert photographs of an illicitly embracing couple; 'All you need then is the official of a foreign power in a compromising situation'.[16] Promoting a miniature Minox 'spy' camera, the feature was published in a climate of spy-mania; the first Bond film, *Dr No* had just been released and the Vassall case was in the headlines. Such ocular allegories of photography and spying – of surveillance – multiplied and folded back into self-reference for Morley when he was commissioned to illustrate the jacket for Noel Behn's novel, *The Kremlin Letter* (1967) (fig. 12). His photographic design showed a rifled secret dossier of official state papers and the paraphernalia of spy iconography (Luger pistol, hypodermic syringe). Amongst them Morley included an inset photograph, a version of Christine-in-the-chair, but with face cropped. The photograph within the photograph was a mirrored reminder of the scandalous narrative surrounding his first photograph of Christine which had been purloined from his studio and covertly published in the *Sunday Mirror* (fig. 10).[17] Disclosure within an aura of the illicit, a reckless unveiling to the public gaze of the body out of place; this theme structures many of Morley's productions.

From the jacket cover of *The Kremlin Letter*, from amongst the display of 'secrets' a camera points at the spectator. For some time the imagery of the target had been commonplace in British Pop painting: one of the *Private Eye* artists, either Barry Fantoni – an ex-RCA contemporary of Pauline Boty – or William Rushton, had produced a design for the Establishment Club of a target with an eye, unblinking at its centre. It was coolly described in 1962 in *Town* magazine; 'Comment on cannibalistic England: "Private Eye Is Watching You", announces a large poster in the "Establishment". What can they be watching? Themselves'.[18] Morley photographed the sign during a fine display of narcissism by *Private Eye* staff during the shooting of a French fashion advertisement four years on. The 'eye' is simultaneously target and with its stunted *homunculus*-like legs and hands, an aggressive watcher.[19] An apotropaic eye, too, to ward off the miasmic authoritarianism of the British Establishment in the realm of its 'low' other, the Establishment Club, an eye to oversee and spy back upon it. With the seemingly impeccable Tory Establishment credentials of its personnel – its proprietor, Nicholas Luard, for instance; Winchester and the Guards – the club in the sleazy heart of Soho was an exemplary site of carnival confusion between the boundaries of 'high' and 'low'.

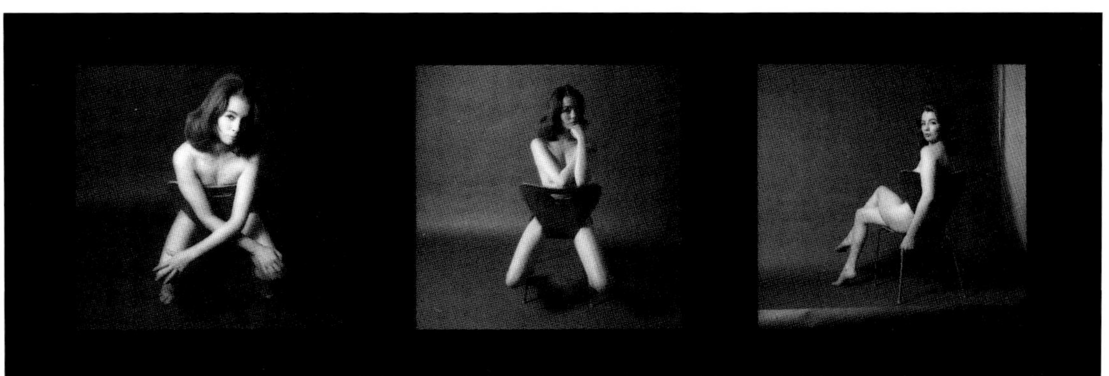

13 **Christine Keeler**, contact sheet, 1963

The Hidden Zany

Their faces hidden, the mythical 'Man in the Mask' and the 'Man in the Leather Apron' were at the centre of tantalizing rumours of an occluded world of power and perversity during the summer of 1963.[20] Allied motifs of grotesque concealment animated Morley's portrait of the *Private Eye* contributor and ventriloquist of fundamentalist male Conservatism, John Wells (no. 66). But carnival laughter breaks in, for the photograph turns on the notion of mute media deprivation; his head is in a paper bag, deaf to the radio he holds to his ear; he is also unseeing through the perched glasses. In his anonymity he is the Invisible Man of the Transistor Generation, a sixties grotesque: – not a part of those cheerful craft and folk vestiges of grotesquerie that Morley photographed at the fairground in his 1959 feature, but the advent of some monstrously comic satiric creature.

Rubbish and the Fringe

Many of Morley's portraits traffic in this monstrousness: John Wells again lolls, tumbled down, slumped, all awkward legs, posing as the ludicrous 'journalist' Manfred Fysh (but in fact parodying David Hockney's recumbent sprawl) in Morley's *Private Eye* tableau of May 1965, 'Some of the Young Pacey People Who Make London Swing'. The mock gathering was a travesty of the *Weekend Telegraph's* assembly of artists and culturati.[21] The others present gawp around a slashed metal junk sculpture with multiple openings. This is the newly carnivalized social body of 'Swinging London', and it appears distinctively marked by what Bakhtin dubbed 'grotesque realism': '... images of the human body as multiple, bulging, over- or undersized, protruberant and incomplete. The openings and orifices of this carnival body are emphasized, not its closure and finish ...'.[22] The base and the low were embraced in Morley's carnival; he had photographed the junk sculptor Bruce Lacey and his bizarre band, The Alberts, who performed at The Establishment Club on Monday evenings,[23] recording their *Evening of British Rubbish* at the Comedy Theatre. (He collaborated with them in stage design as well). The genteel was brought low: the imperturbable Kenneth Horne was portrayed by Morley for *She* magazine in a scene of brutalist squalor, stuffed in a dustbin, Endgame-like: 'Summing up his ever immaculate attire ... our photographer decided to dispose of this cantankerous critic'.[24] The socially disgusting and unclean was given priority; for example, when the *Beyond the Fringe* team posed for him on Brighton promenade just before their

West End run in 1961. Standing next to a 'rubbish eater' bin painted with an enormous schematic mouth and implacable teeth, the young Peter Cook feigned vomiting and Dudley Moore imitated the consumption of waste, both with gusto (fig. 14).

Inverted Identities

From scraps of photography Morley made comic photomontages for *Private Eye* covers which inverted the symbolic hierarchies of power and governance, inducing the socially 'high' into 'low' scenarios, interrupting their commodious surroundings with abject circumstances. The excremental metaphors of the grotesque were further elaborated. Sir Alec Douglas-Home, Macmillan's successor as Prime Minister, was shown in photomontage on election eve in 1964, seated on a lavatory bowl (with legs apart, his pose is that of Keeler) demanding by speech bubble that a covering (a vinyl record) be replaced, a barrier restored and decorum reinstated.[25] The monarchy, too, was left vulnerable to this breach in the British symbolic system, and the Duke of Edinburgh's head was spliced by Morley to that of a 'low', down-and-out derelict, a beggar.[26]

Deconstructing the Classical British Body

The palimpsest strategems of collage now seem to be a major, if unacknowledged, resource for artists working across a range of disciplines in Britain in the early sixties; a format which could promise to resolve the severe ills and discontinuities of a post-imperial culture. The Establishment Club took to mixed-media presentations reliant on the Berliner Ensemble's staging devices (seen at the Royal Court theatre in the late fifties) and *TW3* extended this direction even more successfully. Joe Orton conceived his literary style as being a form of collage,[27] referring to his play

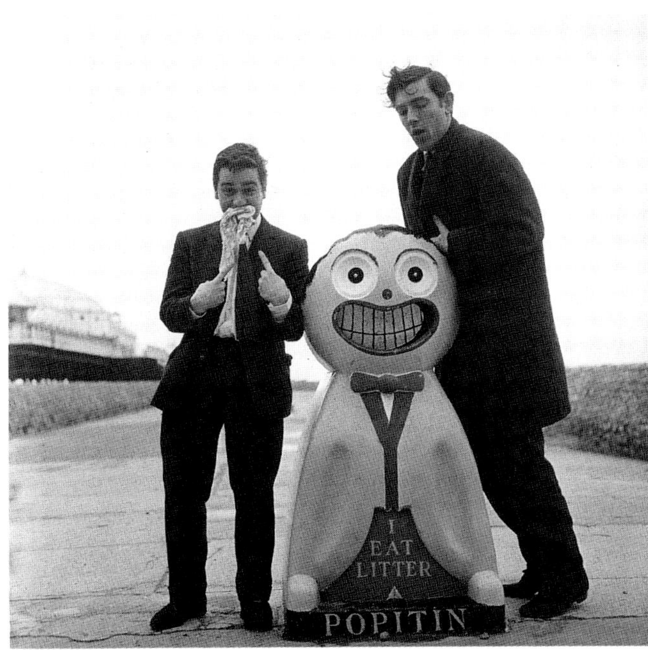

14 **Beyond the Fringe: Dudley Moore and Peter Cook**, 1961 (no. 62)

Entertaining Mr Sloane (1964) which Morley photographed. He had also been gaoled (in 1962) for his grotesque, *détourné* photomontages of library book jackets. His sitting to Morley, late in 1965, produced a series of nude portraits similar to those of Christine Keeler more than two years before (fig. 15; nos. 91-3). His mock-serious body building was fixed in that 'tasteless' gendered typing of pop iconography; a 'muscleman' to Christine's 'pin-up': the same types inscribed into British pop culture by Paolozzi and Hamilton during the previous decade.[28] Morley's entire career was constructed from his position of difference and antipathy to something we might call (modifying Bakhtin) the classical British body, a repository of *kalokagathia*, of nobility. This is a poised, refined, vertical, distinctly upper middle-class entity, one staged in decorous circumstances: we glimpse it in Morley's ironic portrait of the tall and erect Tinka Patterson flanked by labourers (fig. 16). Like Orton, Morley shifted the boundaries and identity of the body, occasionally with dionysian effects; his publicity shots for the play, *Council of Love* (1970), while part of a larger sixties narrative of the sanctioning of nudity and the obscene, also parallel Orton's anarchy of the body in *What the Butler Saw* (1967).

Rims of Flesh and Hybrids

The grotesque realism of Morley, we might say, 're-opens the body boundary, the closed orifices which normally guarantee the repressive mechanism itself'.[29] How do we see this? As in Francis Bacon's account of the body as undifferentiated meat, the mouth plays a certain role. In 1963 Morley photographed Anthony Powell – at first sight a superb incarnation of that 'classical British body' (no. 25). But Morley represented him with his tongue sticking out; only slightly, but enough to form an extra, third lip. The protruberant lip resembles a piece of photomontage, a rim

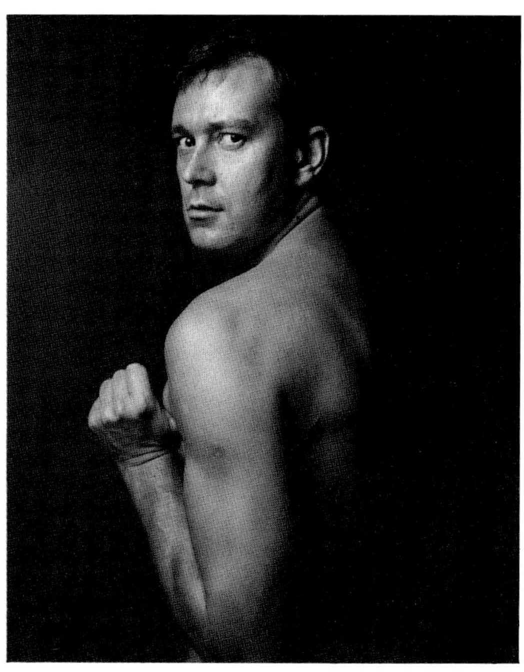

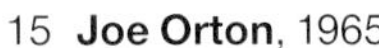
15 **Joe Orton**, 1965

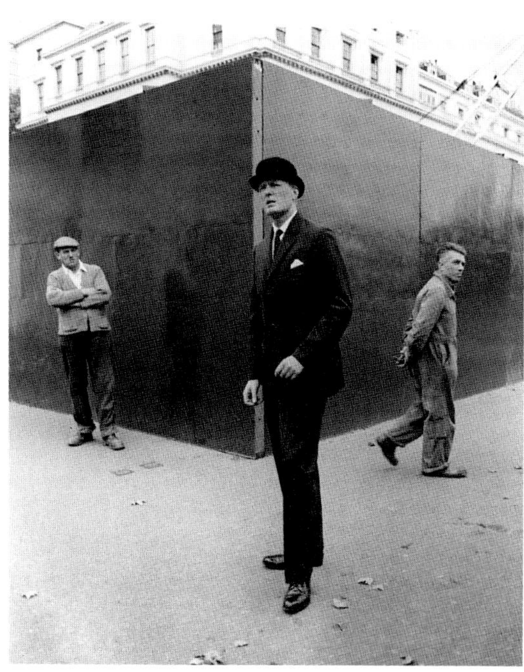

16 **Tinka Patterson** (no. 83)

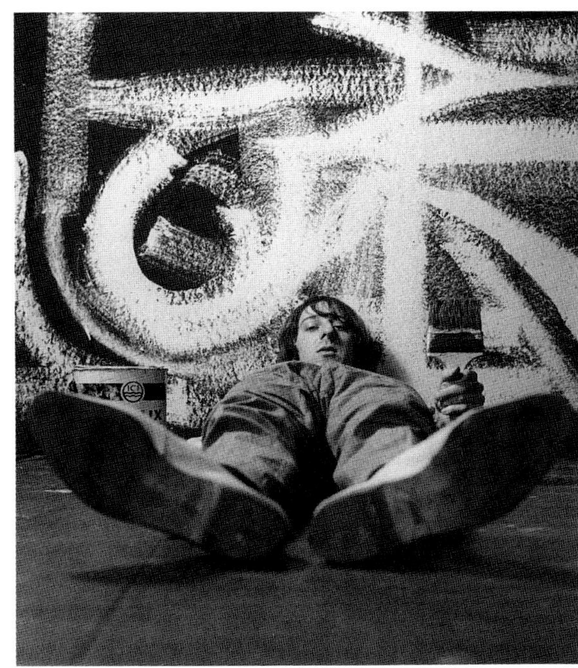

17 **Barry Fantoni** as 'Larry Flies', 1967 (no. 74)

of fleshy matter at a key body opening, an excess which newly re-codes Powell along the registers of grotesque realism. The pop singer Donovan, in 1965, like Anthony Powell, has acquired an excess of flesh; but more gross, with extra folds and layers about his eyes – by condensing his fingers and face into a demonic thing – and thereby swelling those orifices to elephantine proportions. Meanwhile, Bernard Levin sits upright but with a graceless yawp (nos. 68,69): as with Kenny Everett and his wife (no. 46), or the insect-like sunglassed face of George MacBeth (no. 19), some kind of caricatural hybridization appears to have occurred. The bodies of humans and animals burst out in a centreless array in the Kenny Everett portrait, just as Jeff Beck, his Afghan coat, and his hound are all similarly mixed together in an animalizing heterogeneity (no. 54).

Homunculi and Haggard Theatricals

But these sports of nature which Morley has promoted are nothing compared with his two true examples of grotesquerie; Fantoni himself, in the comic guise of Larry Flies the painter (fig.17; no. 74); and Nancy Spain (no. 34). Limbs, body and head are telescoped; Nancy Spain, in a stupifying icon of vanity, is painting her toenails while she is compressed into a body which is simply head, hands and feet; an *homunculus:* – 'disproportionate, exorbitant, outgrowing all limits'.[30] Fantoni is also represented as such an *homunculus*, like the '*Private Eye* Is Watching You' poster, a stunted being. Fantoni, impersonating the fictive Larry Flies in a *Private Eye* lampoon of the colour supplement commodification of artist-as-star, shrinks blasphemously into the posture of Mantegna's Dead Christ. Just so, Peter O'Toole is coded by Morley practising *imitatio Christi*, with a Man of Sorrows' or martyr's countenance. O'Toole's portrait, like those of the playwrights Waterhouse and Hall – who appear on the point of being arrested while checking a script – like

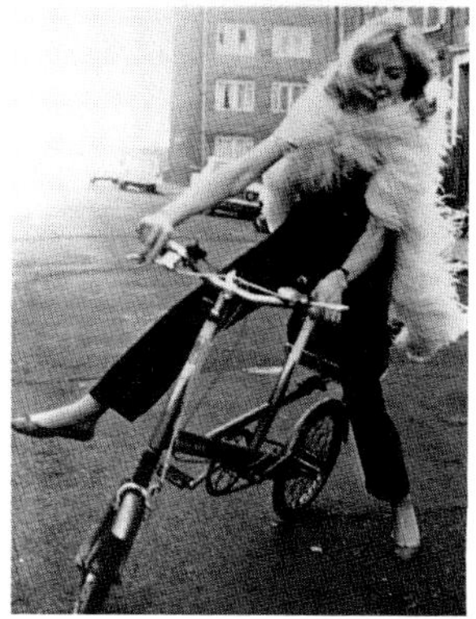

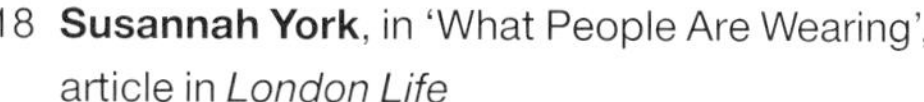
18 **Susannah York**, in 'What People Are Wearing', article in *London Life*

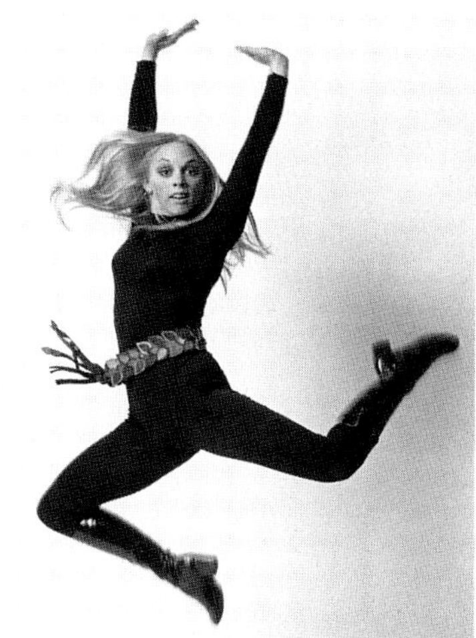
19 **Flick Colby** (no. 84)

John Thaw and other male theatricals, all come before us as haggard, edgy and drawn. While these postures of defensiveness and masochism may have their model in fifties 'rebel' comportments and managements of physiognomy, they speak instead of a type of male heroism and an ego ideal which was under siege and suddenly questionable in the early sixties. This may be best exemplified in O'Toole's contemporary role as the problematic imperial hero in *Lawrence of Arabia* (1962) or in Albert Finney's inadequate male hero of Waterhouse and Hall's play, *Billy Liar* (1960).

Legs and the Woman

Tipping and gawkily falling off her Moulton mini-cycle, Susannah York, as she topples, makes visible the unstable woman's body of the time (fig.18). She is 'all legs': 'Suddenly', commented a writer in *Vogue*, reviewing the past year at the end of 1963, 'legs were the most important part of the body.'[31] These words captioned an Art Kane photograph of a *homunculus*-like model, all legs and forearms, her posture similar (if more impacted) to Morley's Christine. Any developed discussion of the shifts in representations of the re-coded female body in the sixties would have to attend to those leg and lower body signs of jumping, impulsive locomotion and a notional 'freedom'[32]. It is Liz, the running and skipping, 'free' young woman who is the secret hero(ine) of *Billy Liar*. Many representations and especially those of Morley, veer towards carnivalizing women's legs; a 'comic privileging of the bottom half of the body (feet, knees, legs...) over the rational and spiritual control of the head'.[33] It is in this mode that Morley re-stylizes Flick Colby (fig.19) and Mynah Bird (no. 81) – a dancer and a model – as bodies which open and gape in a splaying of legs. With this gesture of the body we have returned to Christine. That apparently contained site of excess, seemingly fixed and barred, is also dispersed, her body radiating in a white, open, inverted letter Y of limbs. From a world upside-down to a word; or to a letter upside-down, that inverted Y is the triumphal disclosure of a scandalous 'toppling'[34] body.

David Mellor

Footnotes

1 See his cartoons of winter/spring 1962-3 collected in Michael Frayn and Bamber Gascoigne (ed.), *The Drawings and Cartoons of Timothy Birdsall* (London, Michael Joseph, 1964).

2 See, for example, Morley's portrait of her with the painting *5-4-3-2-1* (1963) with its fairground numbering.

3 'F for Fairground', *Tatler*, 19 August 1959, pp. 25-8.

4 M. Bakhtin, *Rabelais and his World* (Cambridge, Mass., MIT Press, 1968), p. 109.

5 '...a rowdy form of crowd behaviour, often used against unruly women', P. Stallybrass and A. White, *The Politics and Poetics of Transgression* (London, Methuen, 1986). p. 24.

6 P. Stallybrass and A. White, op. cit., p. 86. This might be the basis for a critical reading of these representations which would disclose the dark verso of this complicit 'satirical moment' and its assumed patriarchalism.

7 Unpublished correspondence quoted in *Pauline Boty,* MA dissertation, Gwyneth King, University of Sussex, 1978.

8 P. Stallybrass and A. White, op. cit., p. 5.

9 C. Booker, *The Neophiliacs* (London, Fontana, 1969), p. 199.

10 See Morley's *TW3* satire on Davis, 'Stubby's Progress', in *That Was The Week That Was* (London, W. H. Allen, 1963), pp. 14-17.

11 R. Barthes, 'Striptease', *Mythologies* (London, Jonathan Cape, 1972), p. 85.

12 See A.L. Urban, 'Keeler, The Photos We Didn't See', *The Australian*, July 1989, pp. 34-8.

13 See the cartoon in *Punch*, 19 June 1963, p. 873; a Covent Garden porter is distracted by a passing woman (Christine Keeler) who is entirely clad in equally scandalous news headlines; similarly, cf. Timothy Birdsall's cartoon of a monster, Rumour, descending with a body made of scandalous headlines on the Palace of Westminster, Michael Frayn and Bamber Gascoigne (ed.) op. cit., p. 28.

14 *Town*, November 1963, p. 50.

15 Ian Fleming, *Casino Royale* (London, Jonathan Cape, 1953).

16 *She*, December 1962, p. 40.

17 *Sunday Mirror*, 9 June 1963, back page.

18 'Town Talk', *Town*, August 1962, p. 5.

19 The design may be a variant of Germano Facetti's cover design for the re-packaged Penguin version of George Orwell's *1984*, re-published in 1962.

20 See Bernard Levin, *The Pendulum Years* (London, Pan, 1969), p. 81.

21 *Weekend Telegraph*, 31 April 1965.

22 P. Stallybrass and A. White, op. cit., p. 8-9.

23 See Jonathan Miller, 'English Rubbish', *Town*, June 1962, p. 44.

24 *She*, March 1962, p. 36.

25 *Private Eye*, no. 73, 2 October 1964.

26 *Private Eye*, no. 208, 5 December 1969.

27 John Lahr, *Prick Up Your Ears* (London, Penguin, 1987), p. 185.

28 See Paolozzi's *Bunk* (*c*. 1954) and Hamilton's *Just what is it that makes today's homes so different, so appealing* (1956).

29 P. Stallybrass and A. White, op. cit., p. 184.

30 P. Stallybrass and A. White, op. cit., p. 9.

31 *Vogue*, November 1963, p. 82, 'Leg Pull'.

32 See David Mellor, 'David Bailey, 1961-66', *Black and White Memories*, Victoria and Albert Museum, 1983.

33 P. Stallybrass and A. White, op. cit., p. 183.

34 This 'toppling' motif of instability has a critical significance in terms of gender, sexuality and representation. See Allen Jones' contemporary paintings of the splayed, falling legs of women/men; their displaced phallicism a consequence of fetishistic barring and male anxieties. Dick Hebdige's reading of Morley's portrait of Christine stresses her as empowered in her 'toppling' – 'Christine Keeler, stripped and shameless, poised to "topple the establishment". This photograph marks the birth of the "Swinging 60s".' ('In Poor Taste', *Block*, no. 8, 1983, p. 65). The motif was summoned up again in the title to the recent *Vanity Fair* article (January 1989) on the film *Scandal* and its publicity simulation of Morley's Christine: – 'The Tarts Who Toppled The Tories'.

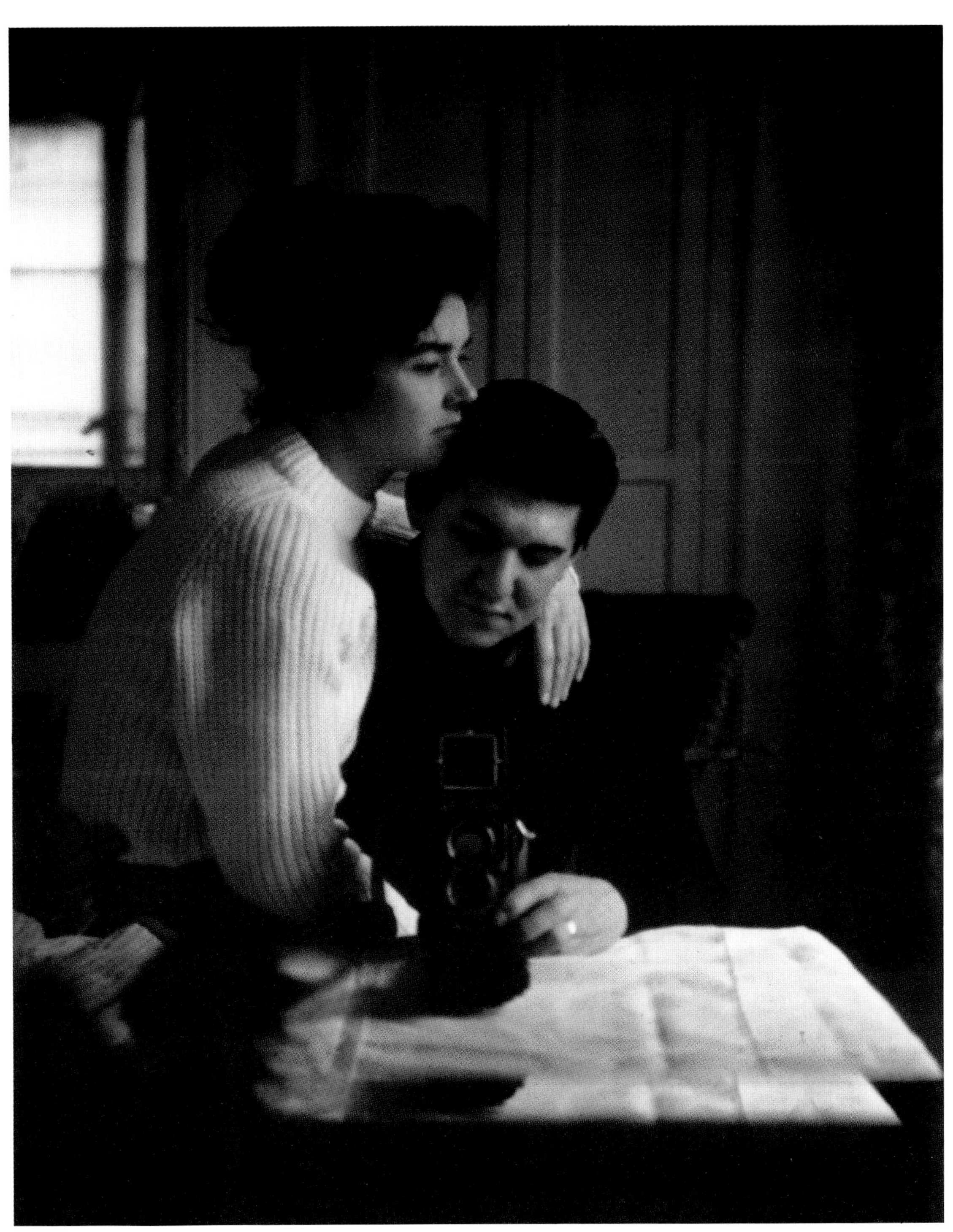

Self-portrait in a mirror with **Patricia Morley**, 1959 (no. 1)

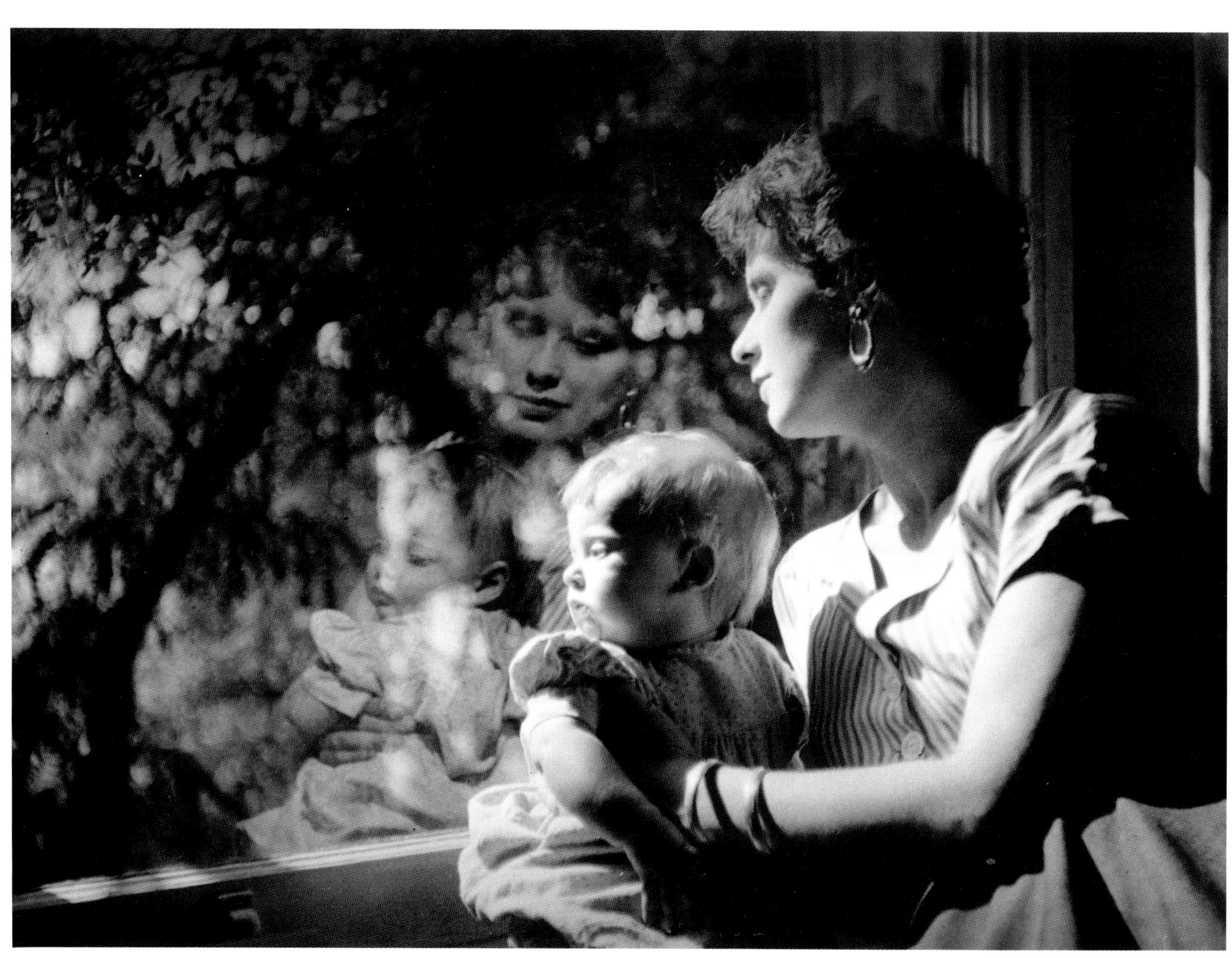

Joan Wyndham and her daughter **Camilla**, 1955 (no. 8)

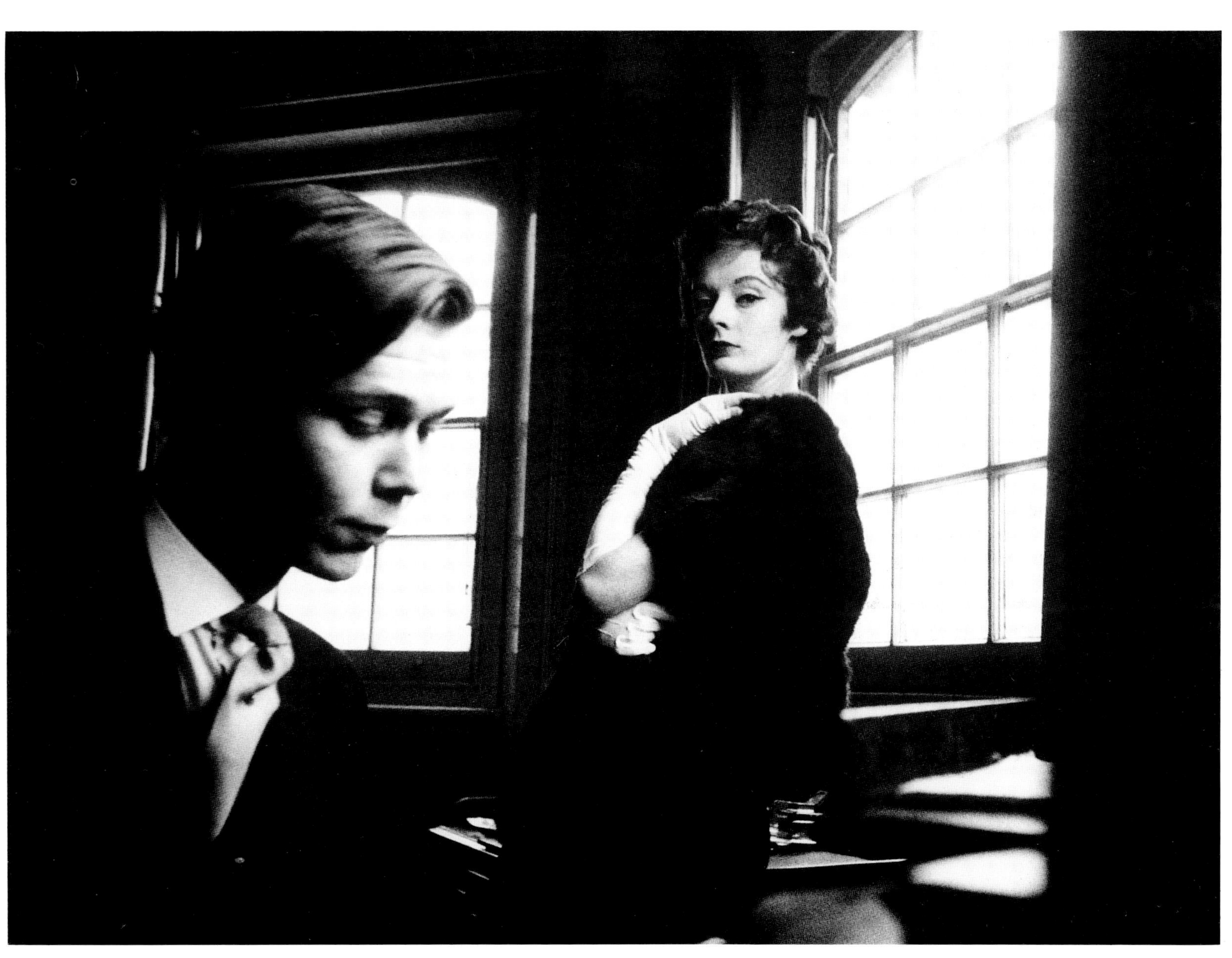

Terry Hamaton, 1960 (no. 9)

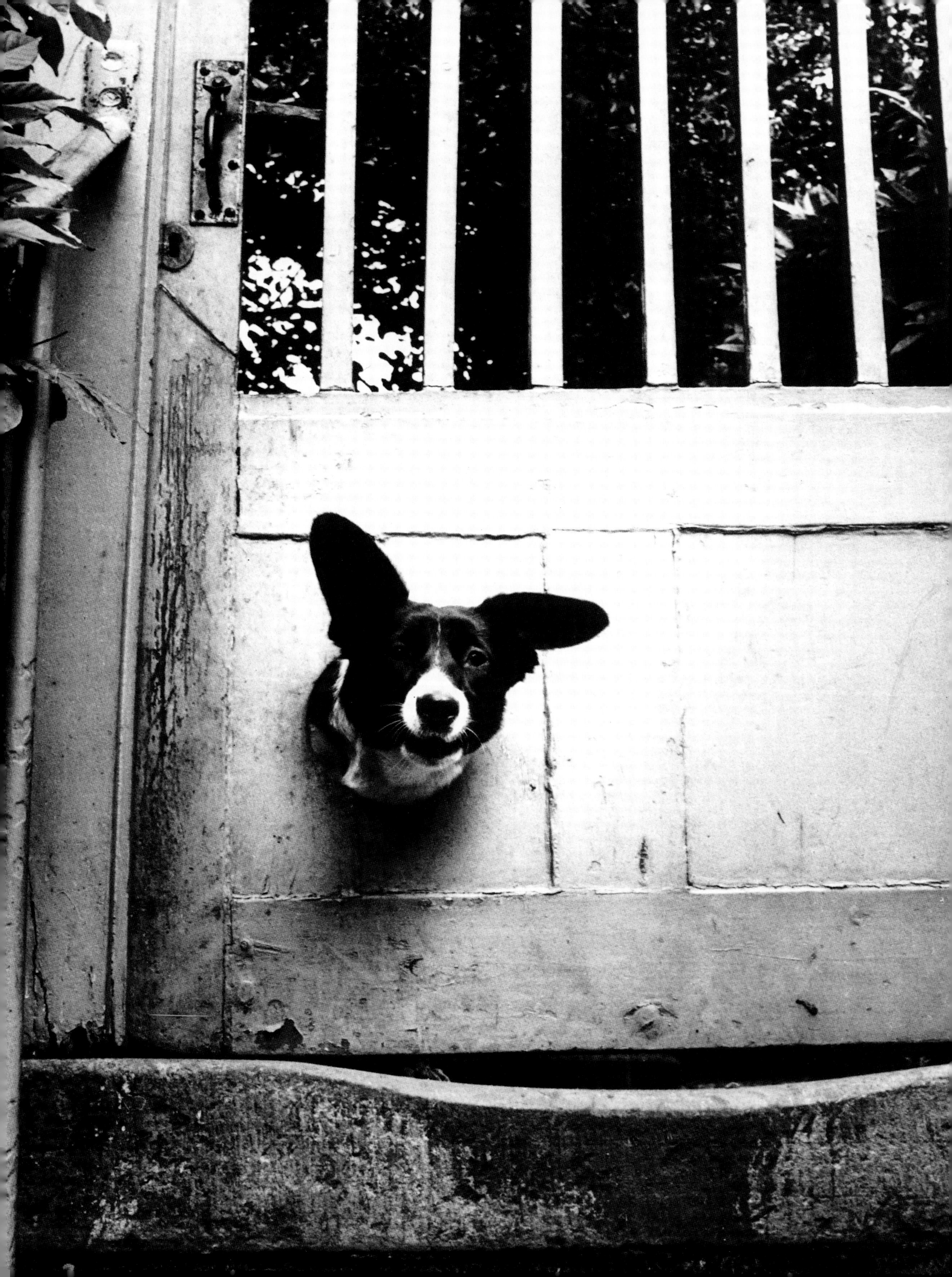

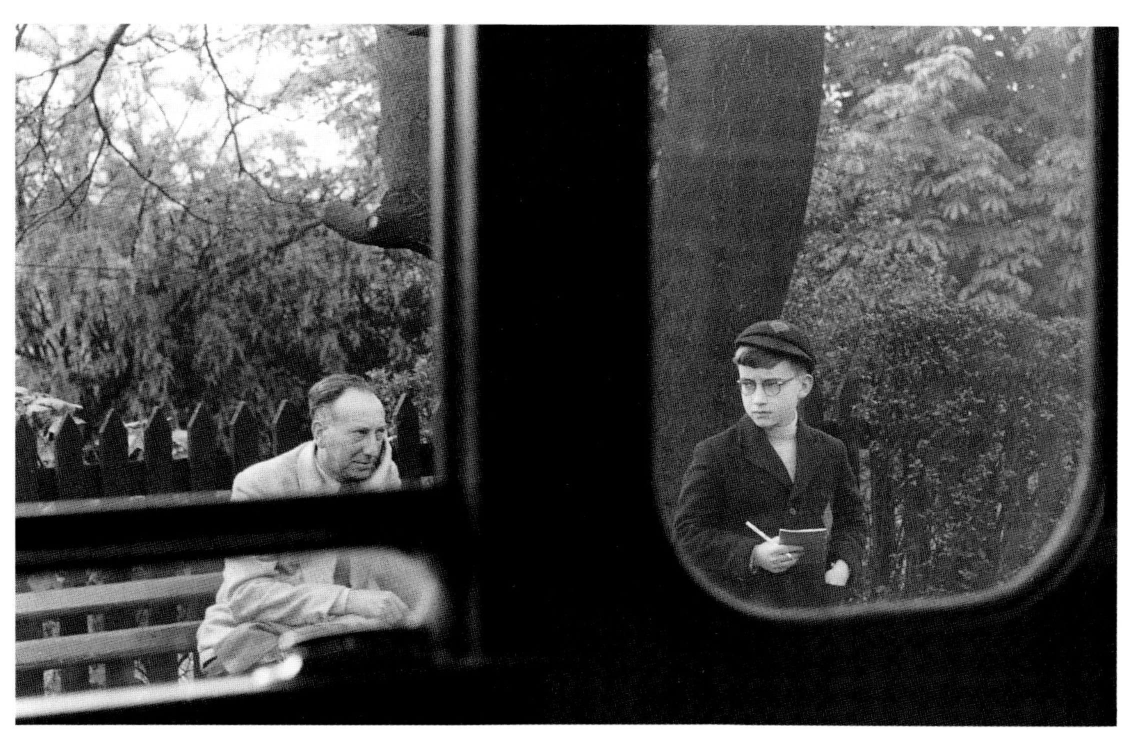

Professor Albert Richardson's dog, 1961 (no. 7)

Trainspotter, 1957 (no. 5)

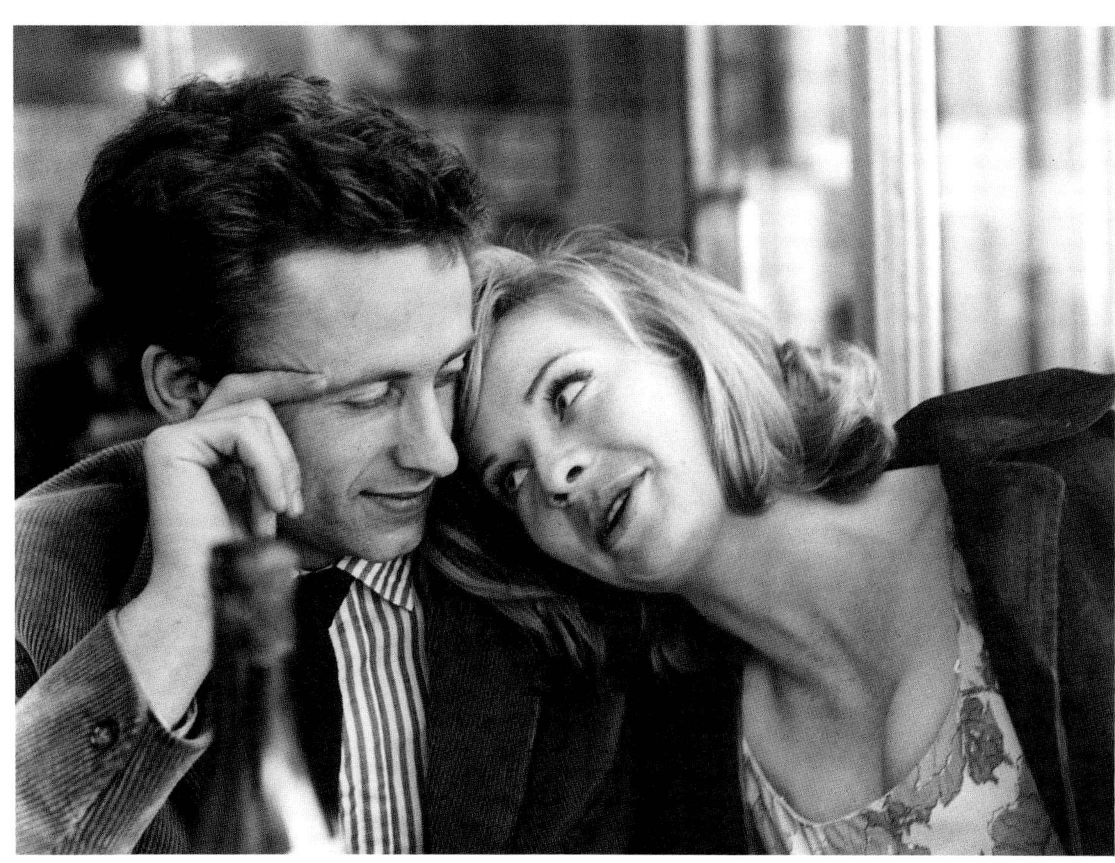

Susannah York and **Michael Wells**, 1961 (no. 36)

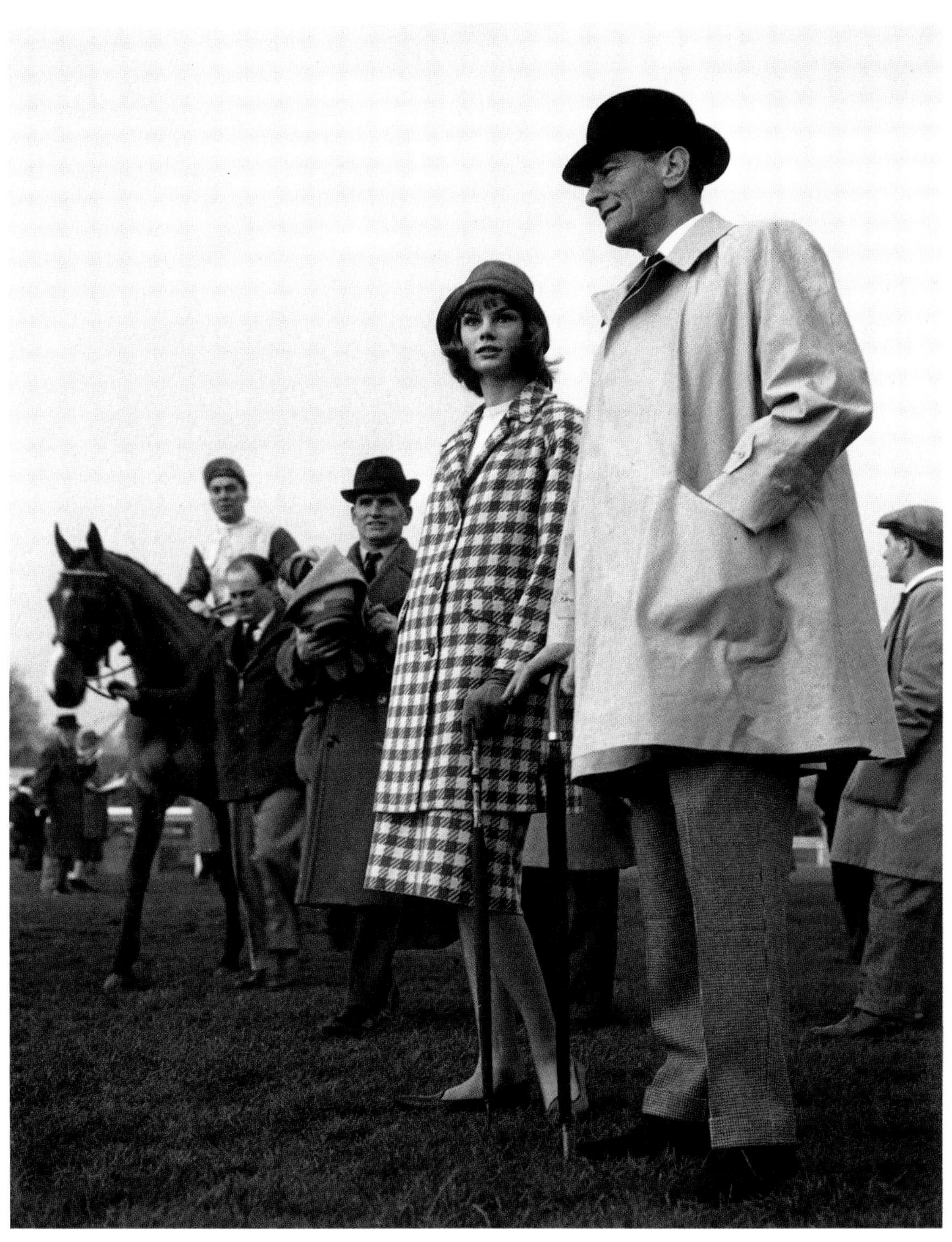

Jean Shrimpton and **Chris Powell**, 1961 (no. 37)

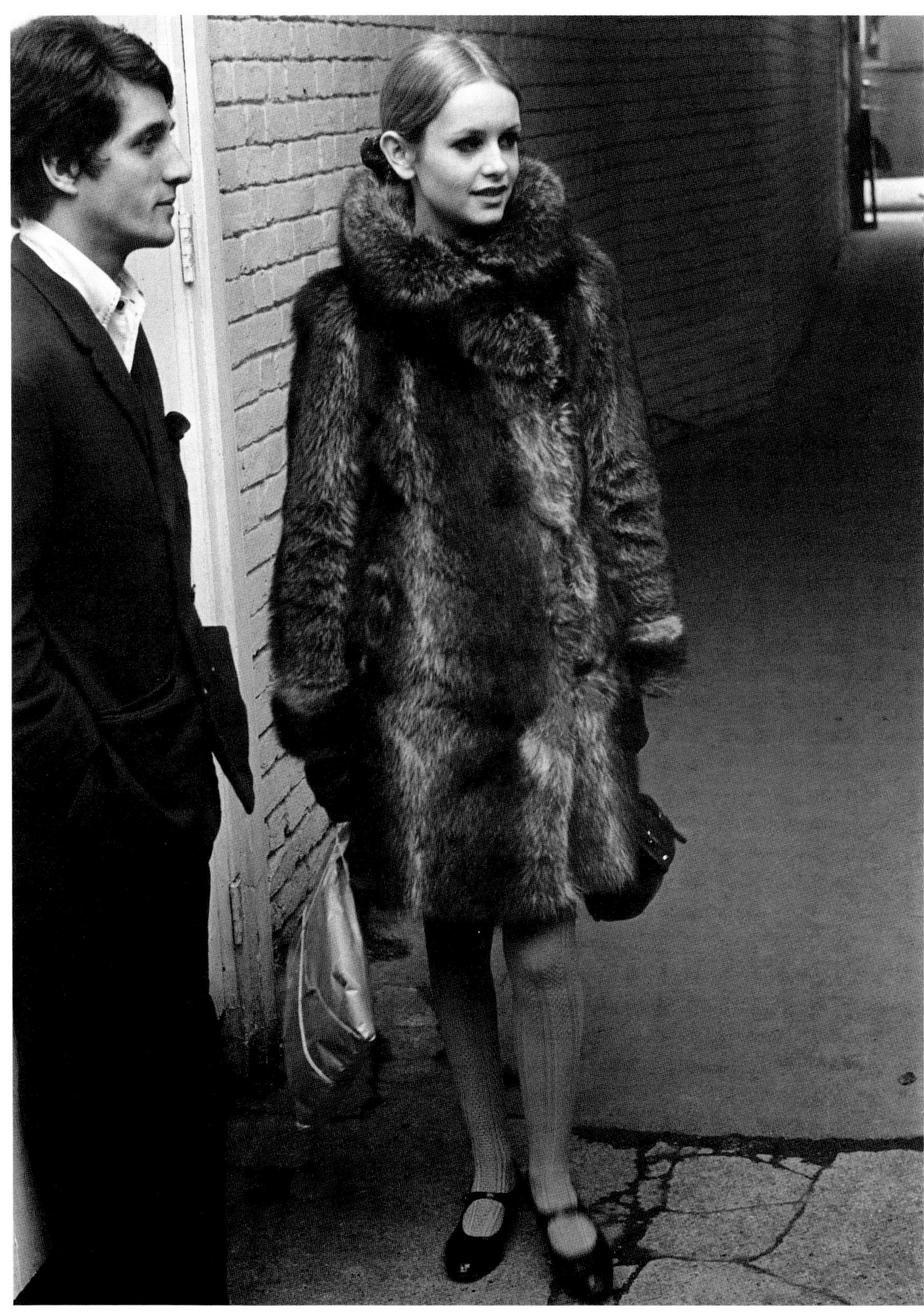

Twiggy and **Justin de Villeneuve**, 1965 (no. 38)

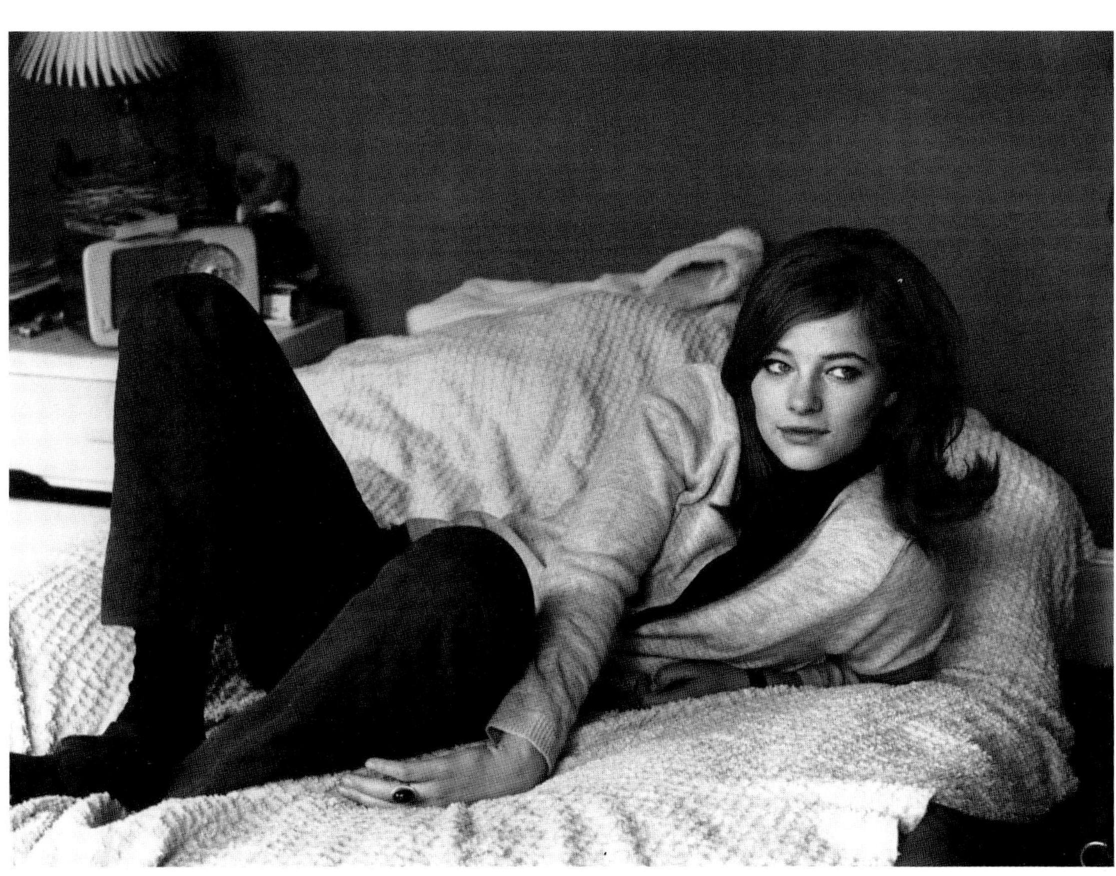

Charlotte Rampling, 1963 (no. 39)

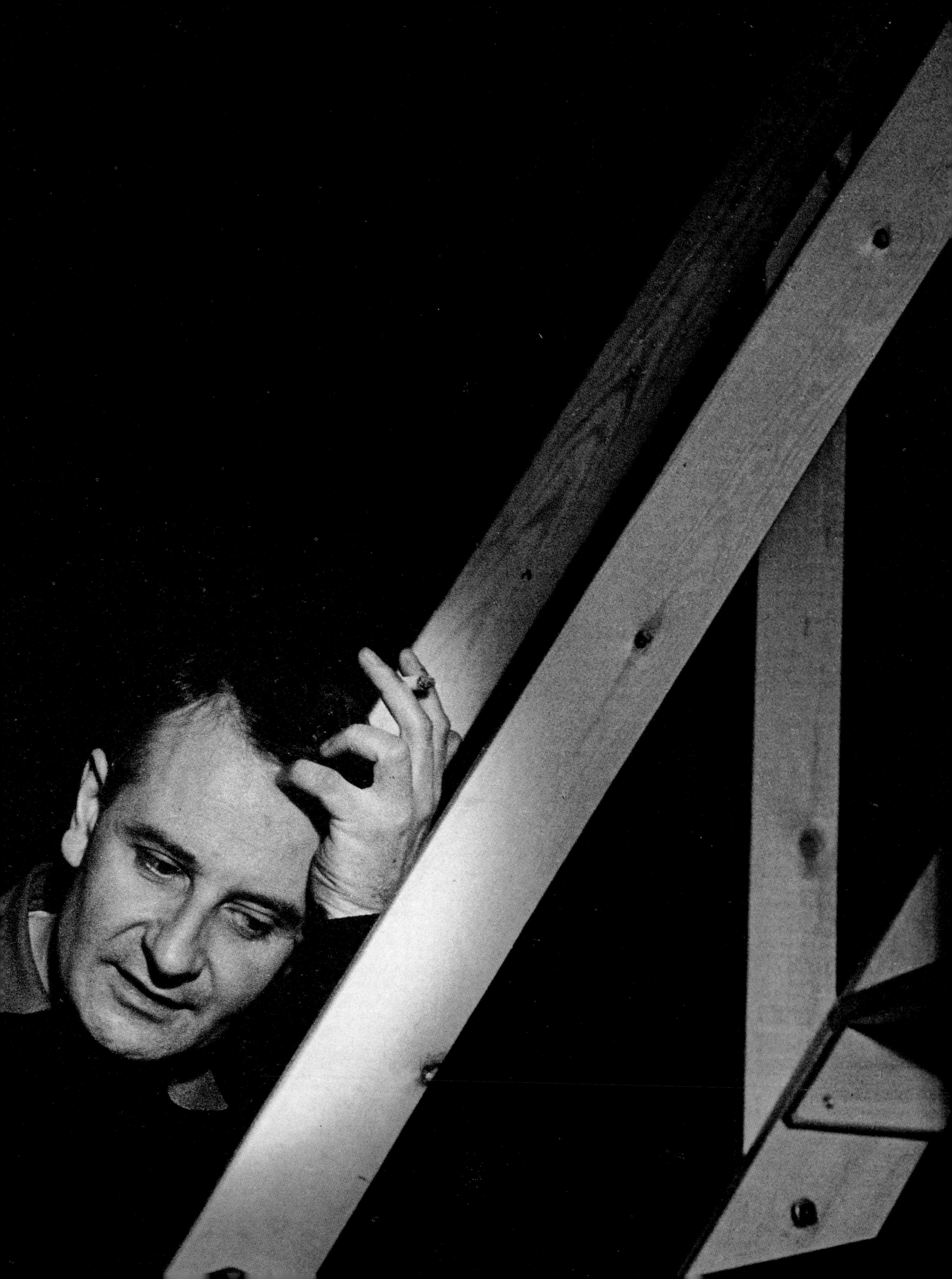

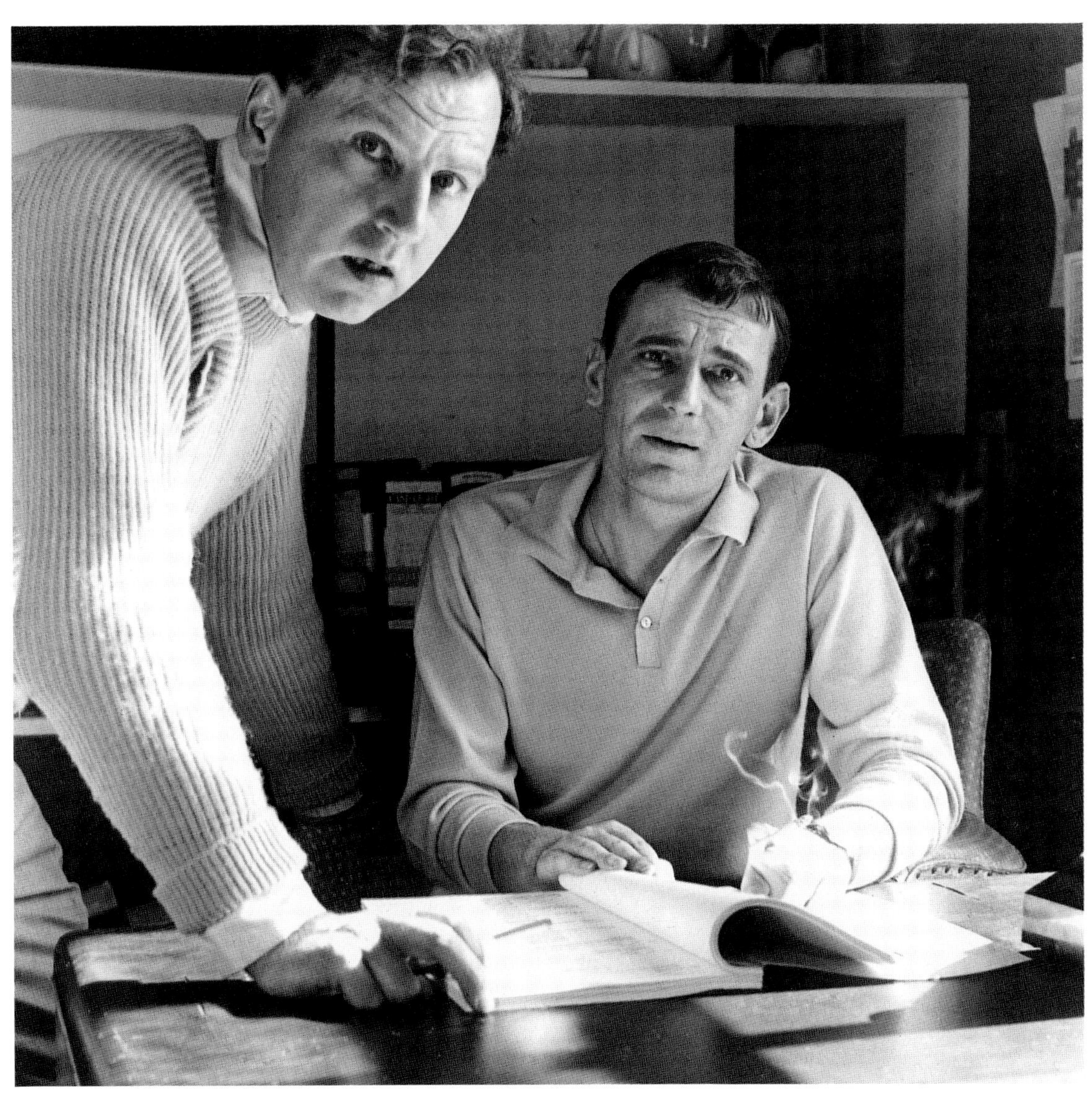

Lindsay Anderson, 1960 (no. 20)

Keith Waterhouse and **Willis Hall**, 1960 (no. 21)

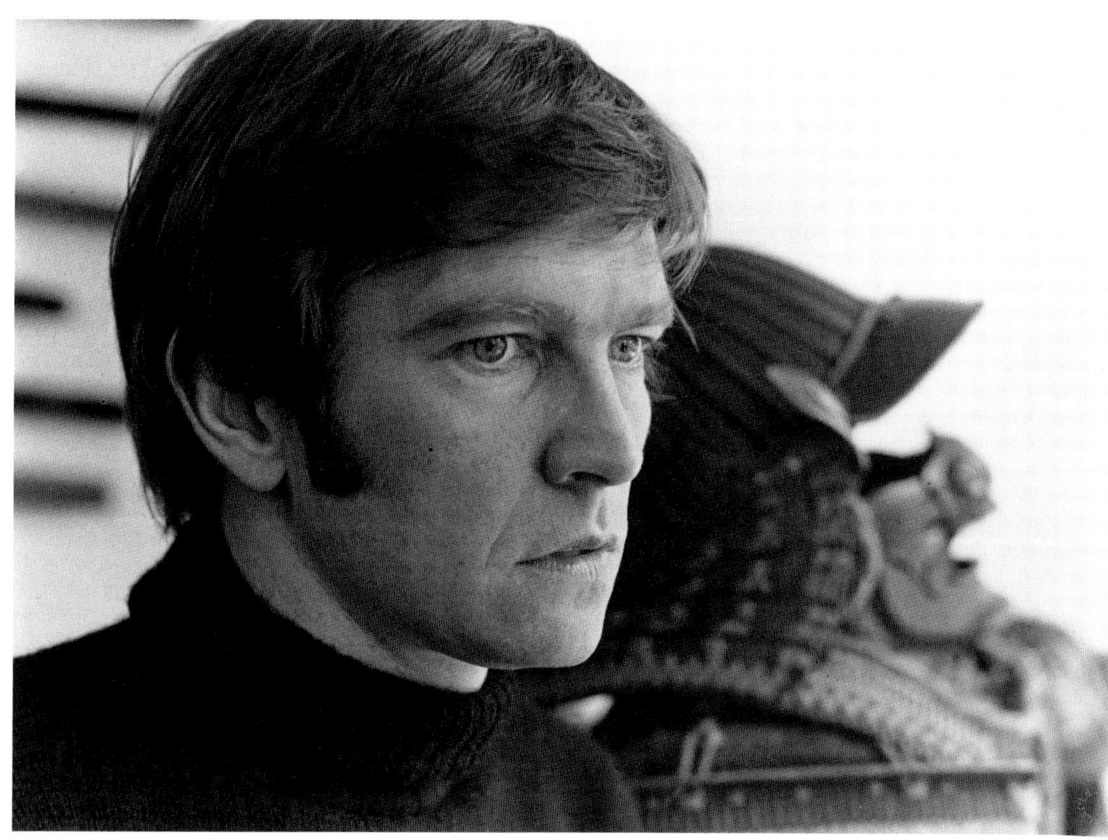

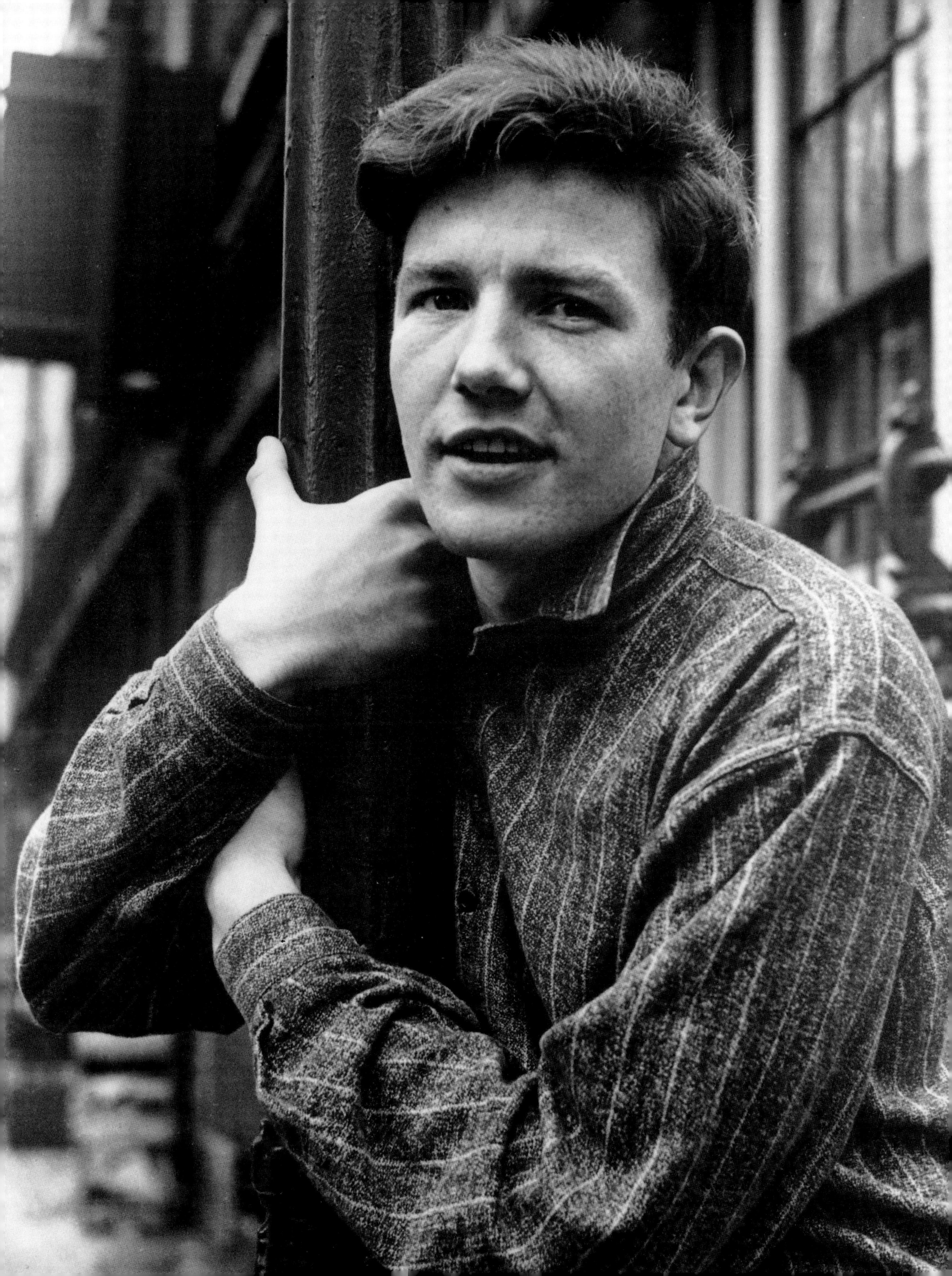

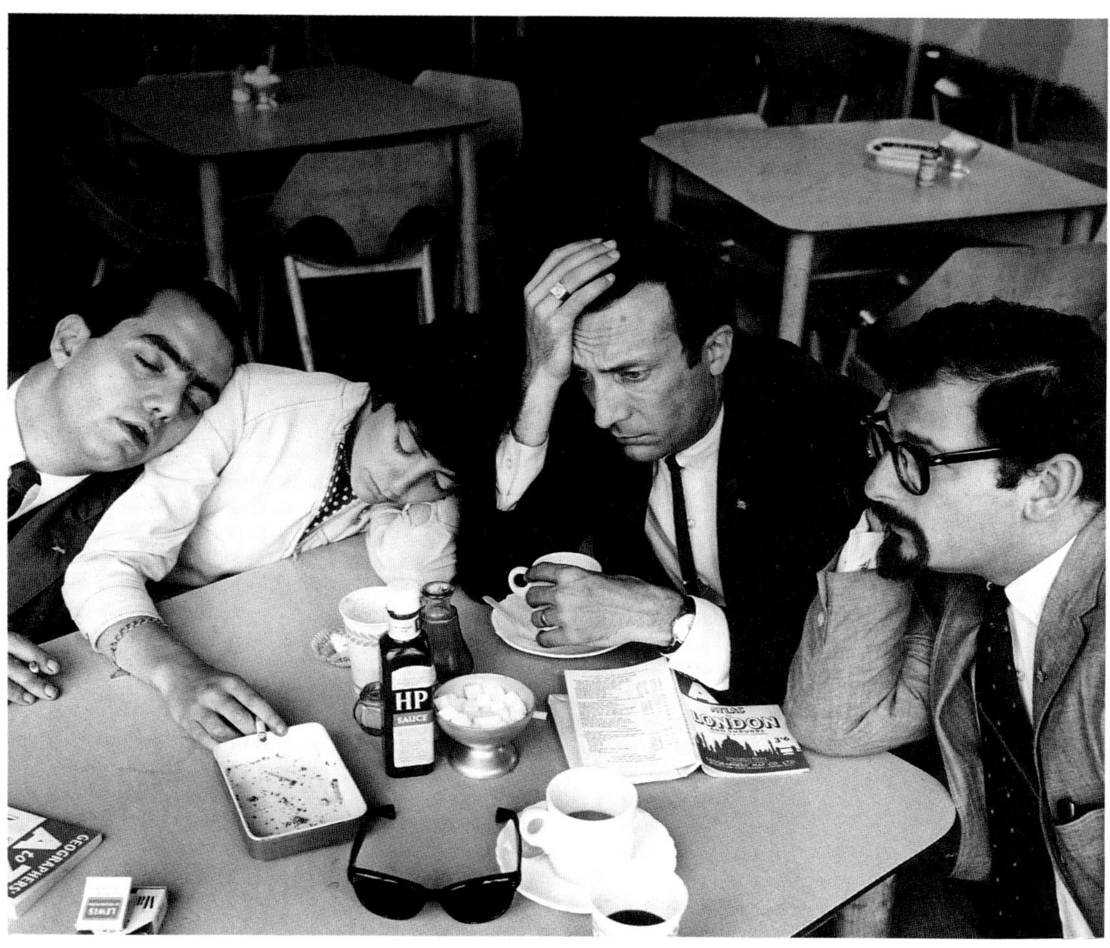

The Premise: Theodore J. Flicker, **Joan Darling**,
James Frawley and **Thomas Aldredge**, 1962
(no. 60)

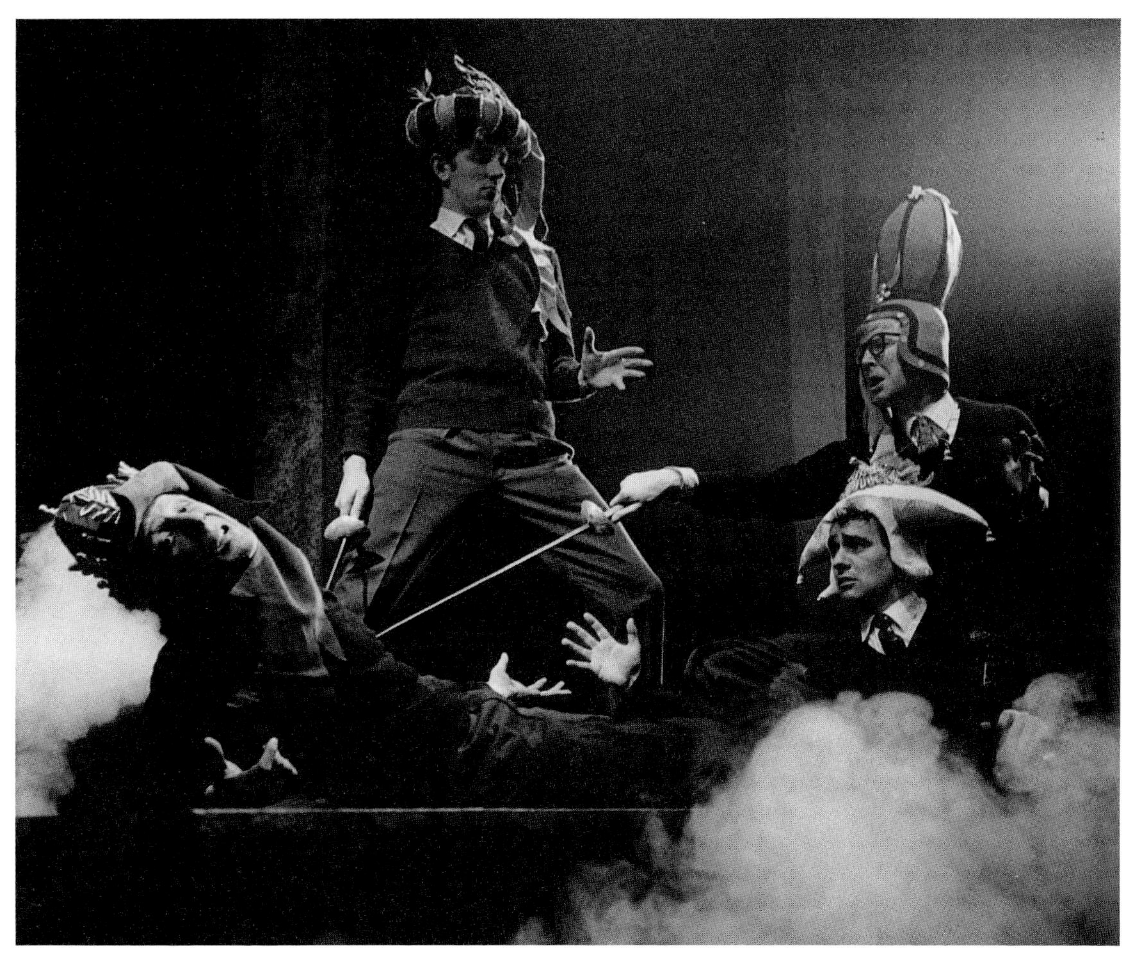

Beyond The Fringe cast: **Jonathan Miller**, **Peter Cook**, **Alan Bennett** and **Dudley Moore**, 1961 (no. 64)

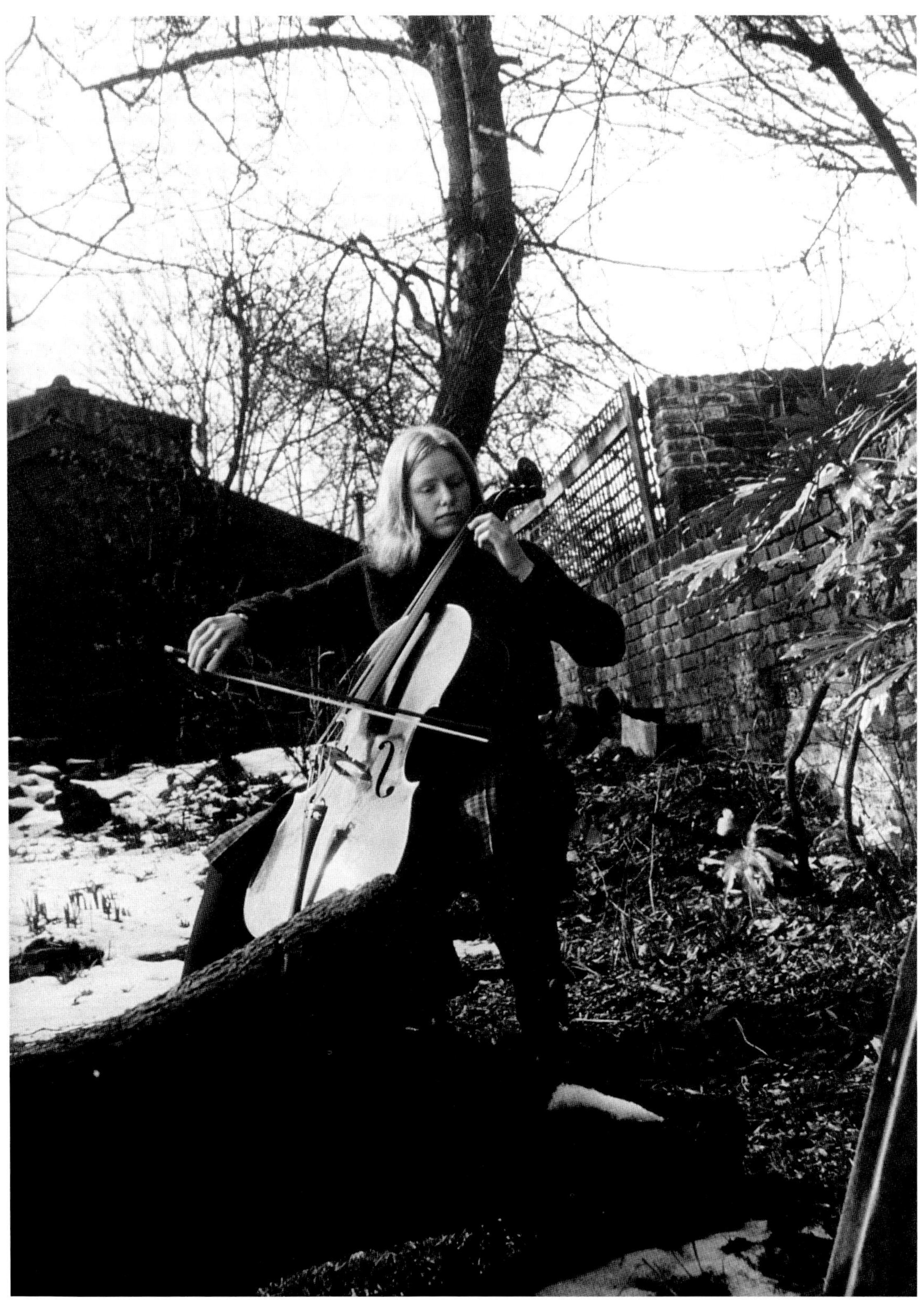

Jacqueline du Pré, early 1960s (no. 14)

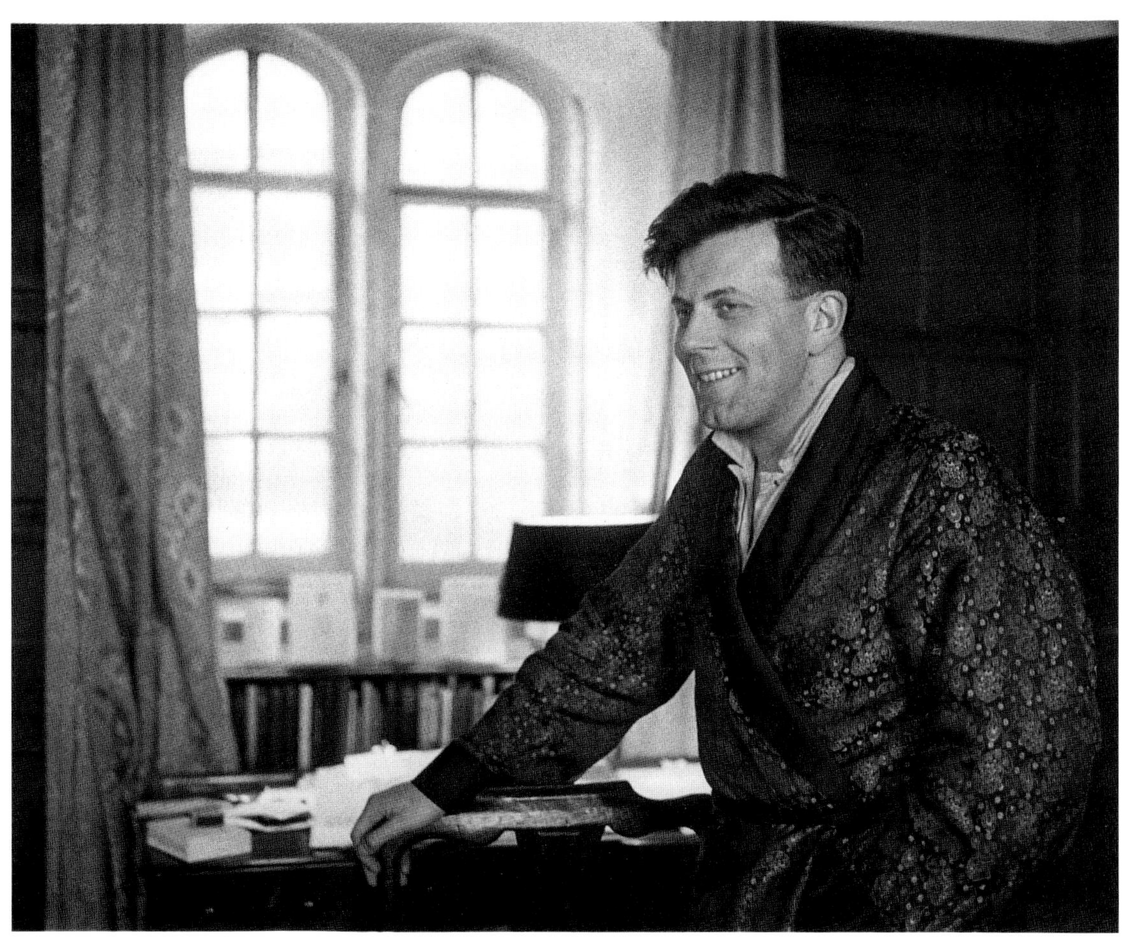

Raymond Leppard, 1960 (no. 15)

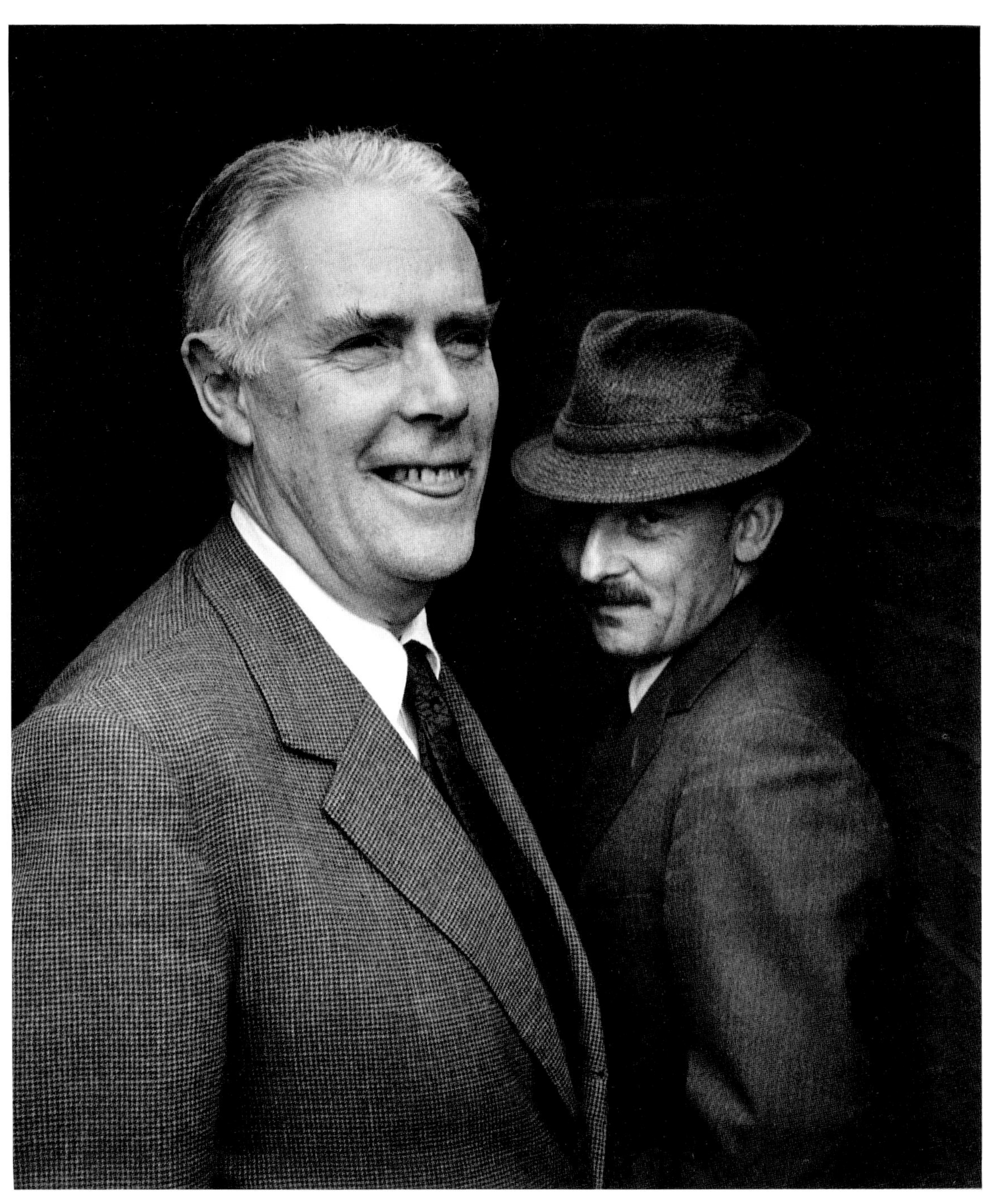

Anthony Powell and **Riccardo Arragno**, 1963 (no. 25)

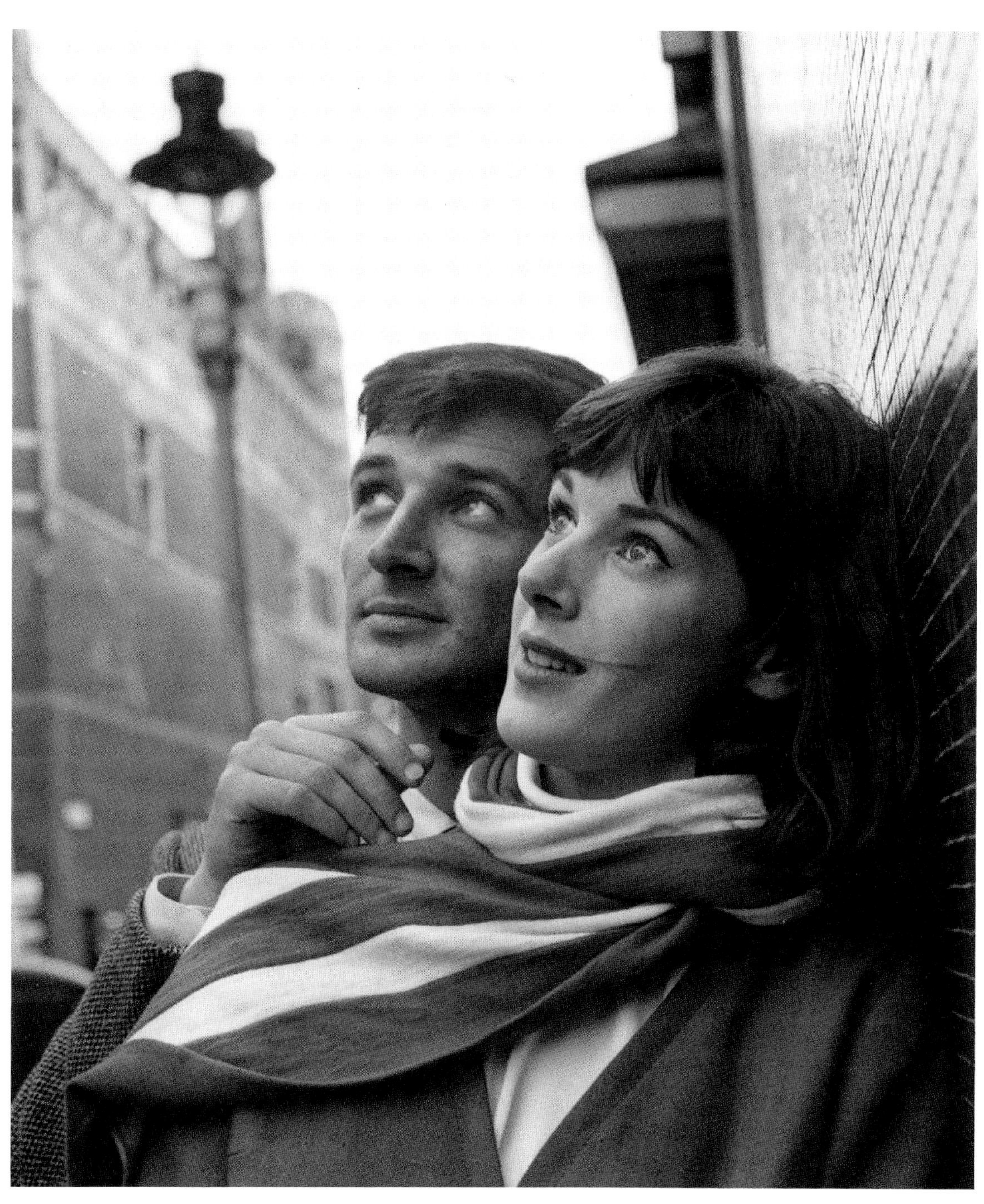

Robin Ray and **Susan Stranks**, 1960s (no. 24)

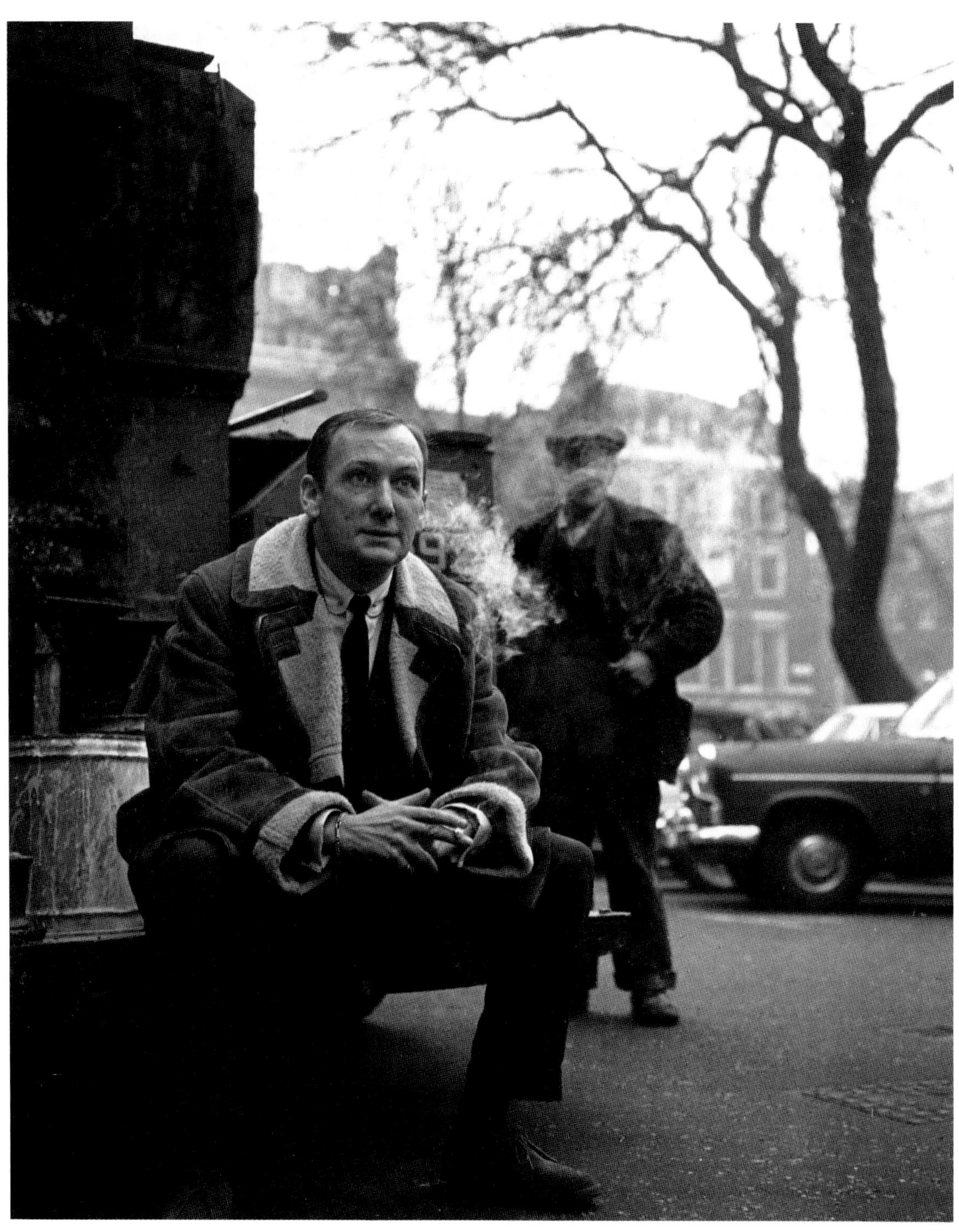

Johnny Speight, 1962 (no. 26)

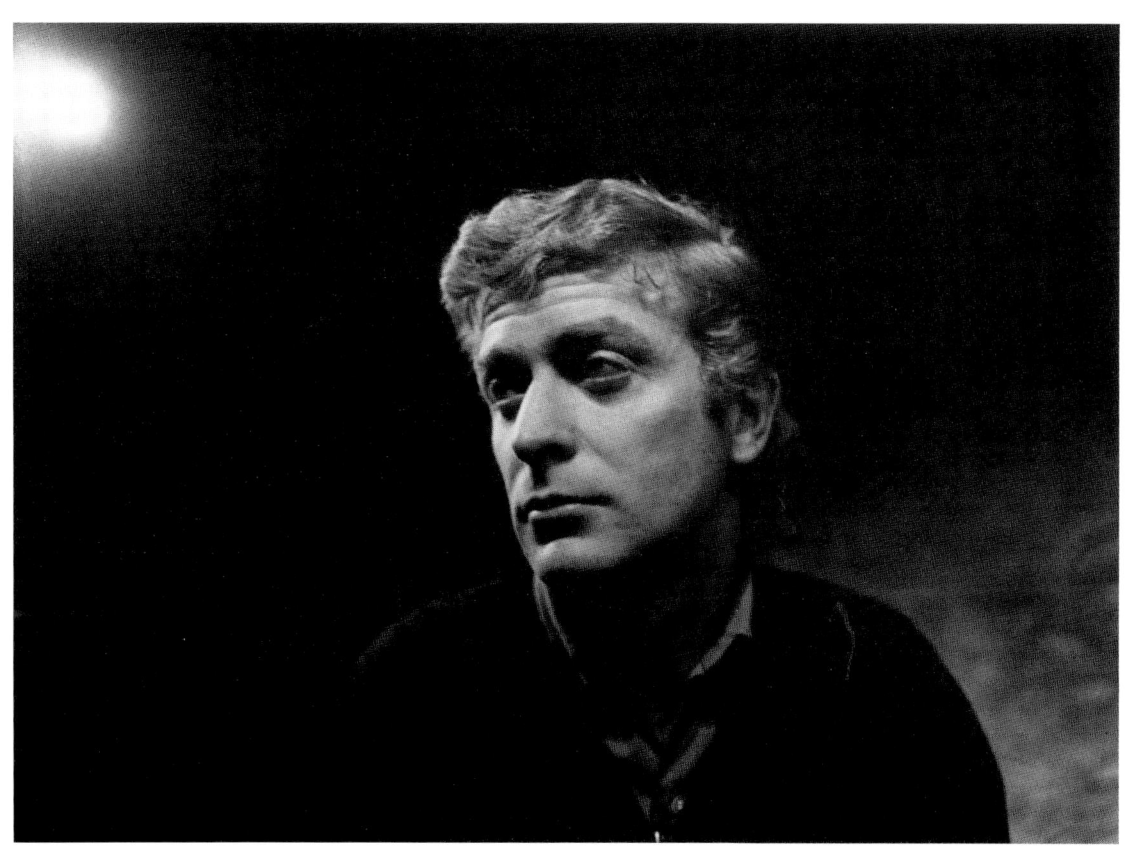

Michael Caine, 1963 (no. 27)

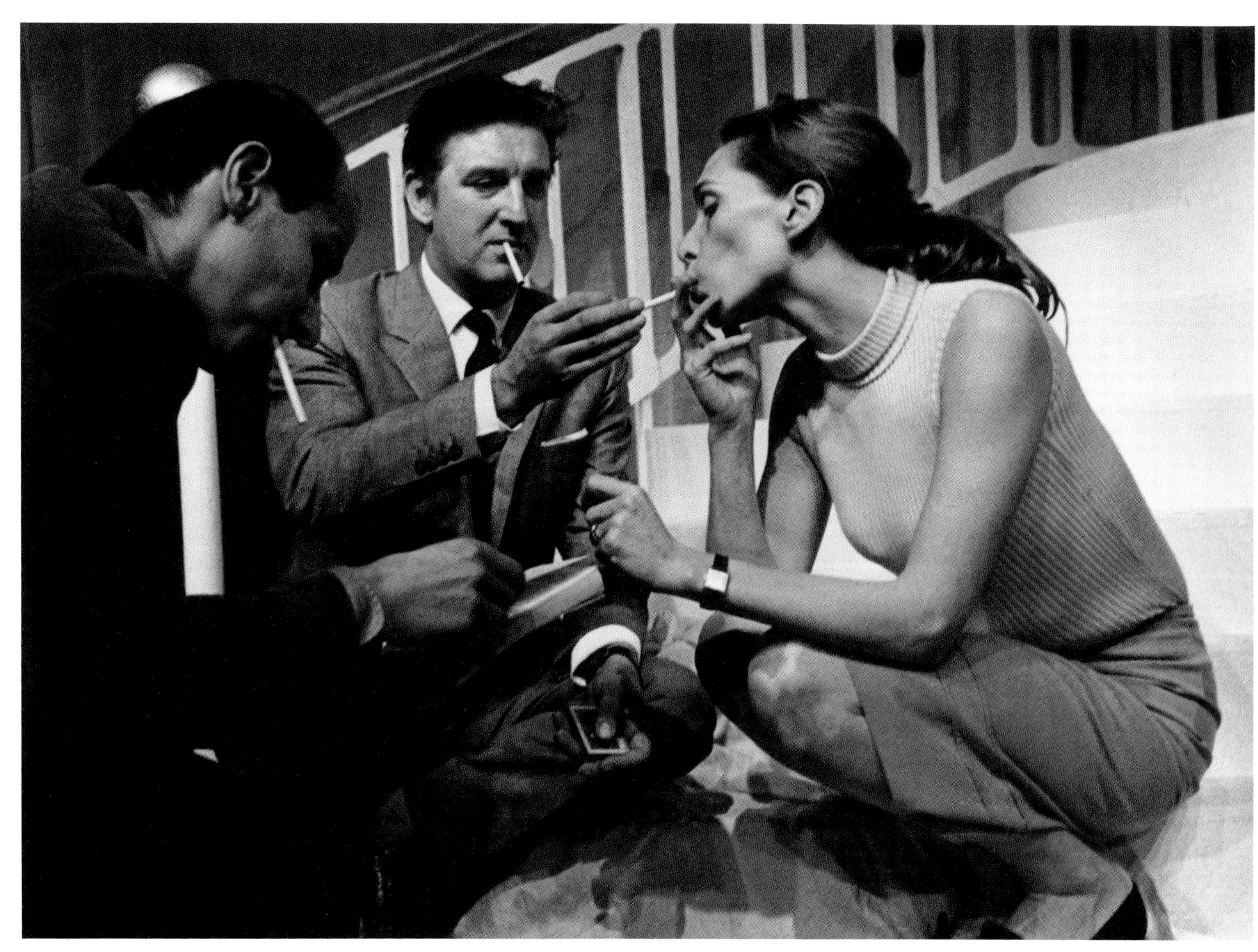

Sian Phillips, **Alan Badel** and **Philip Wiseman**, 1965 (no. 56)

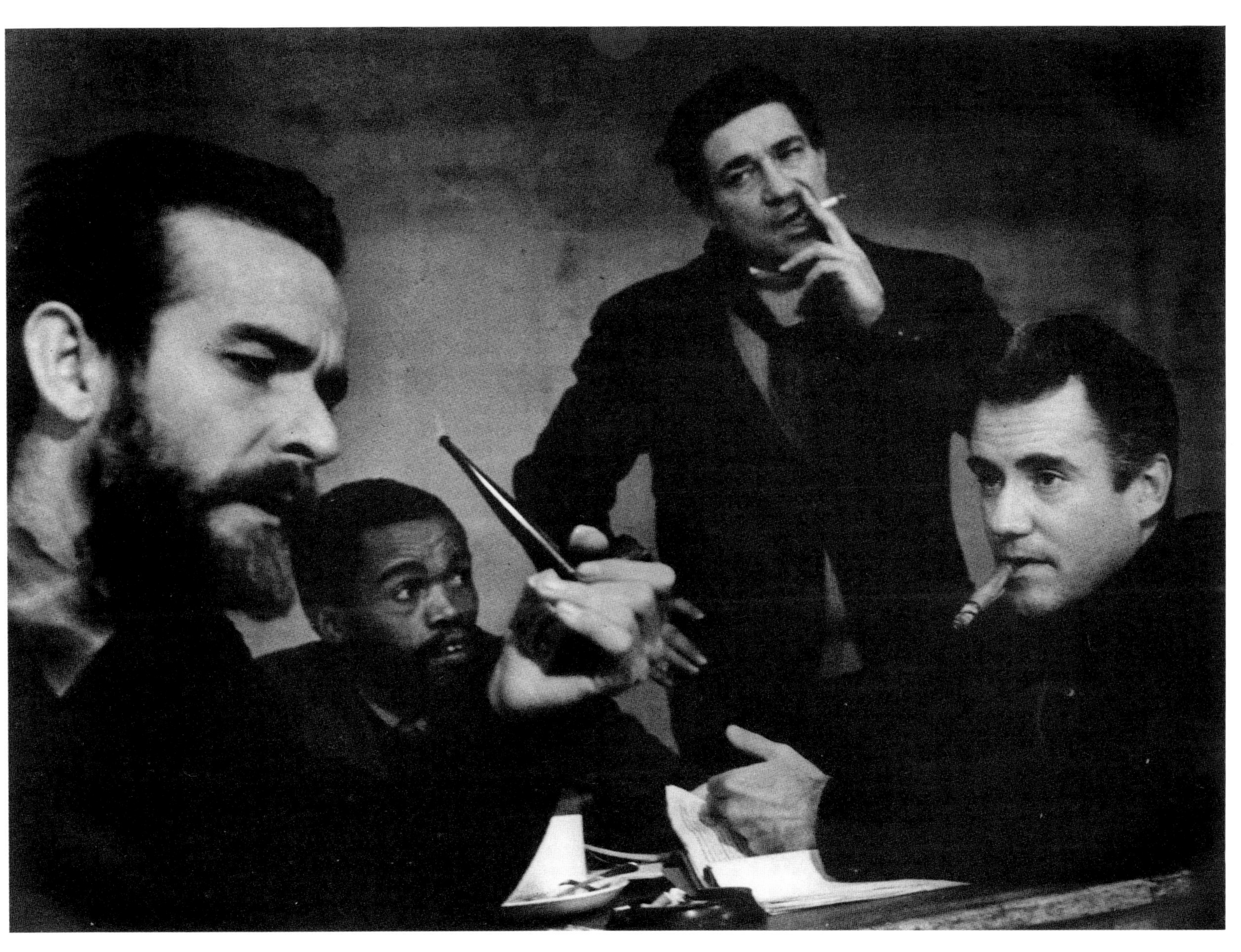

Athol Fugard, Zaikes Mokae, John Berry and **Ian Bannen**, 1963 (no. 57)

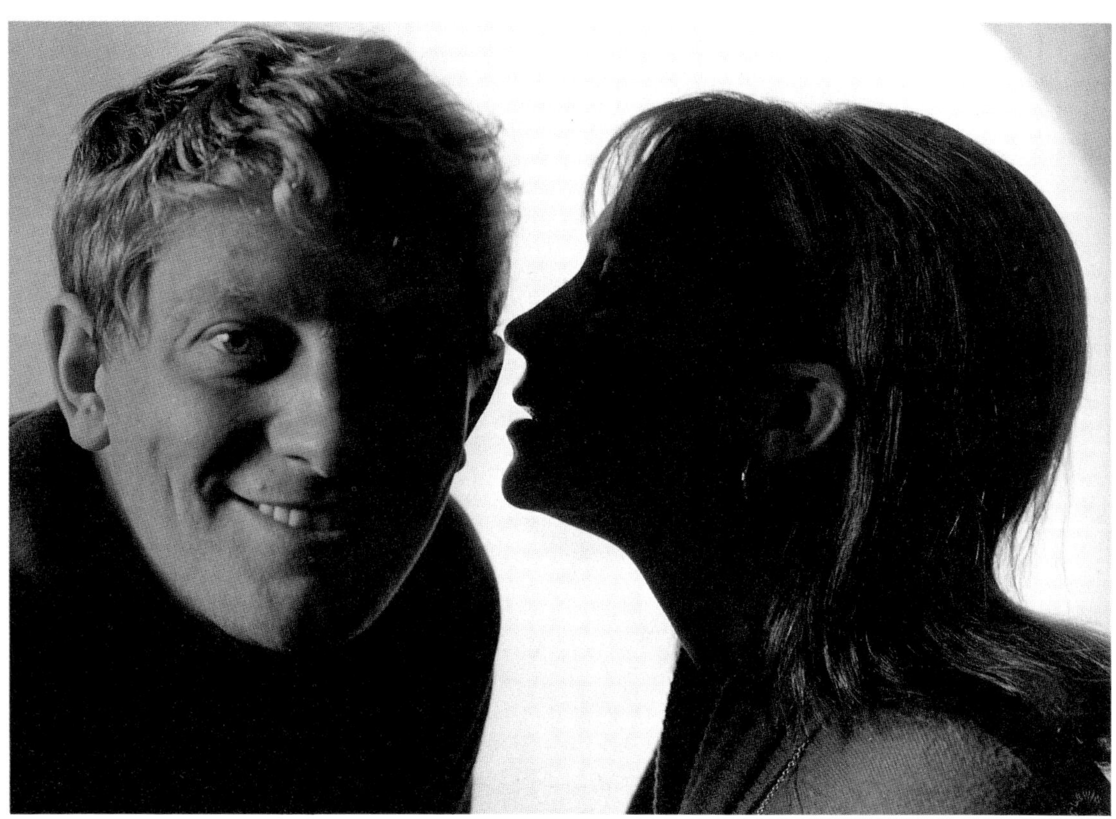

Felicity Kendal and **Drewe Henley**, 1968 (no. 58)

John Cleese and **Connie Booth**, 1968 (no. 59)

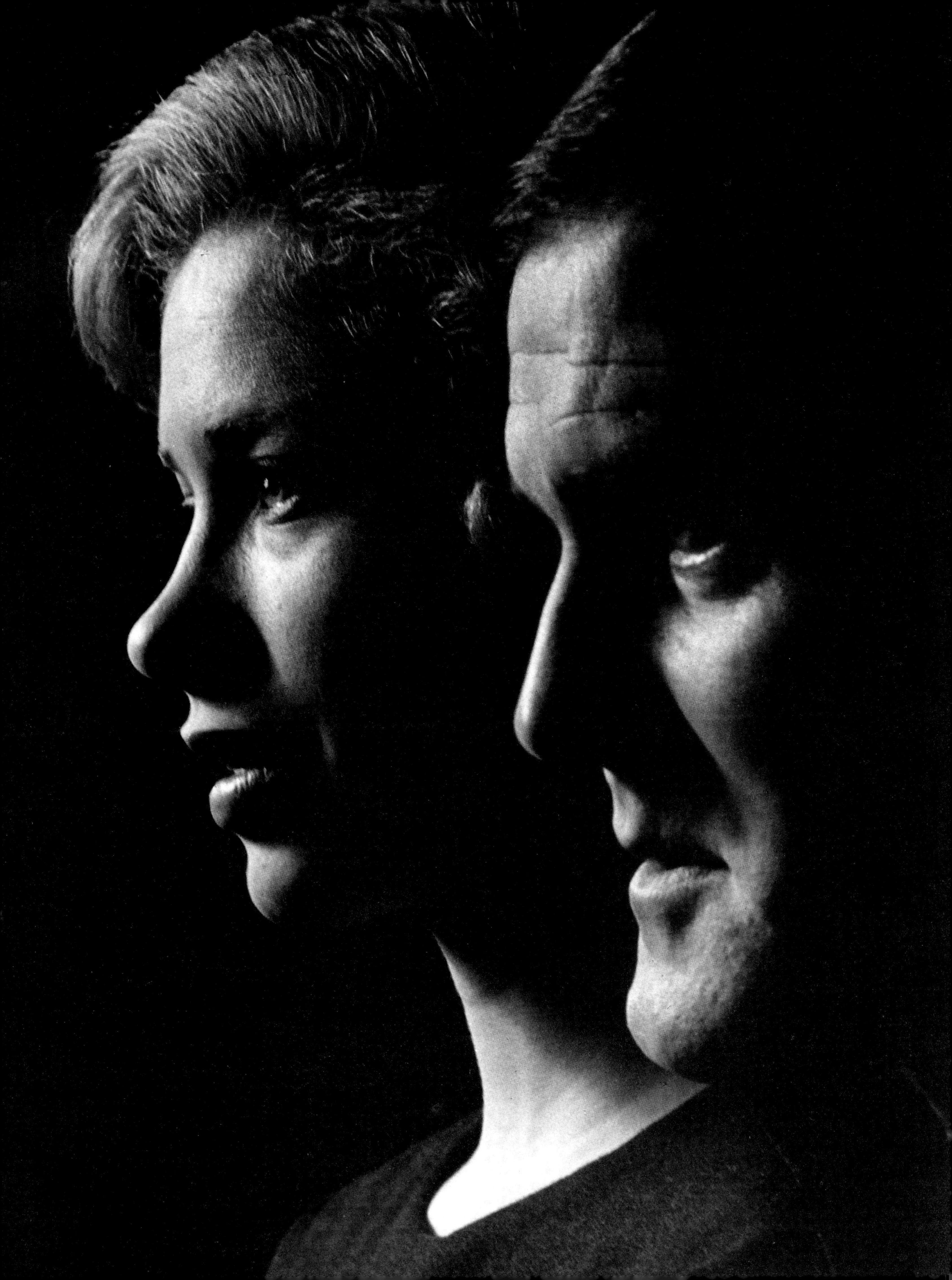

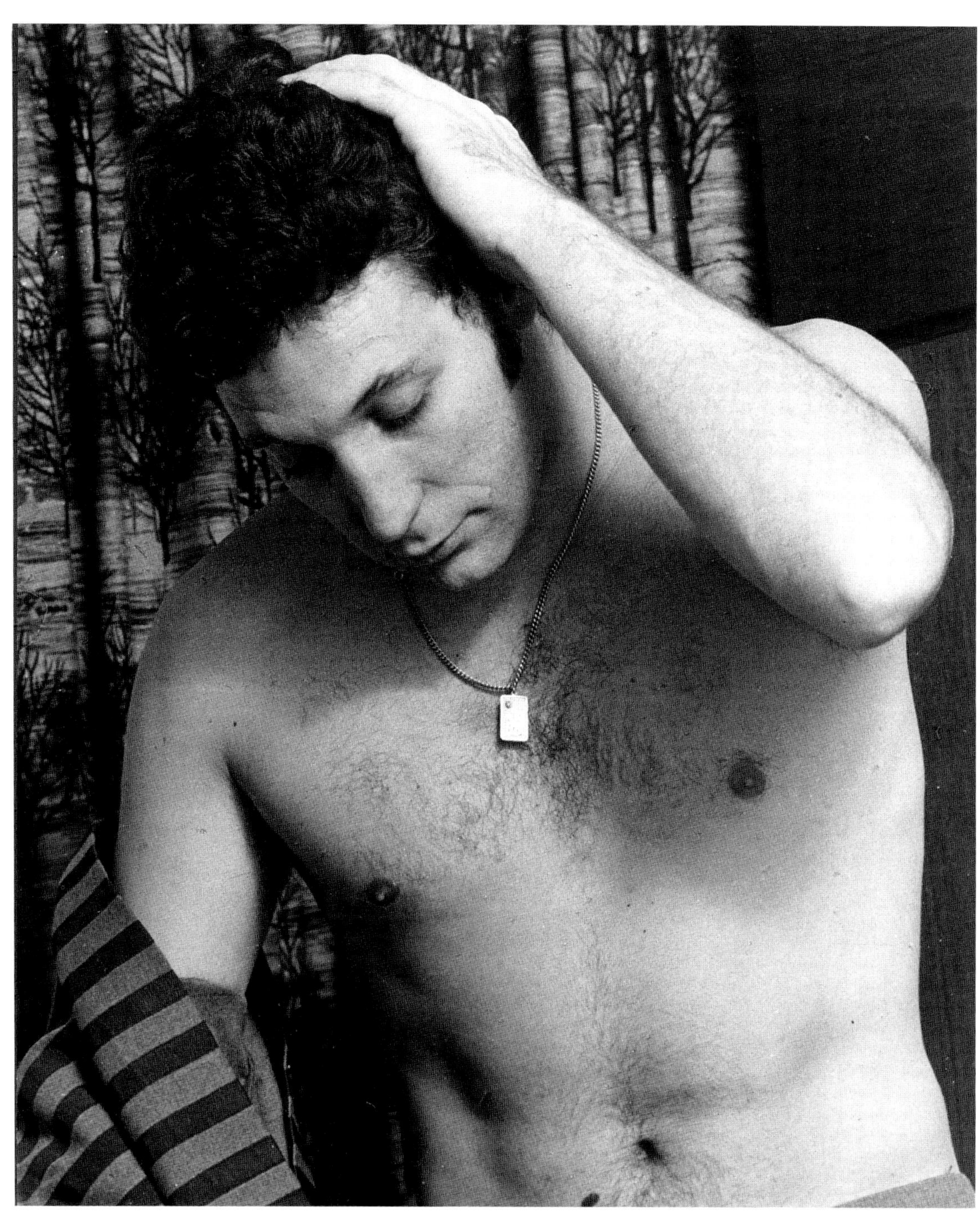

Tom Jones, early 1960s (no. 40)

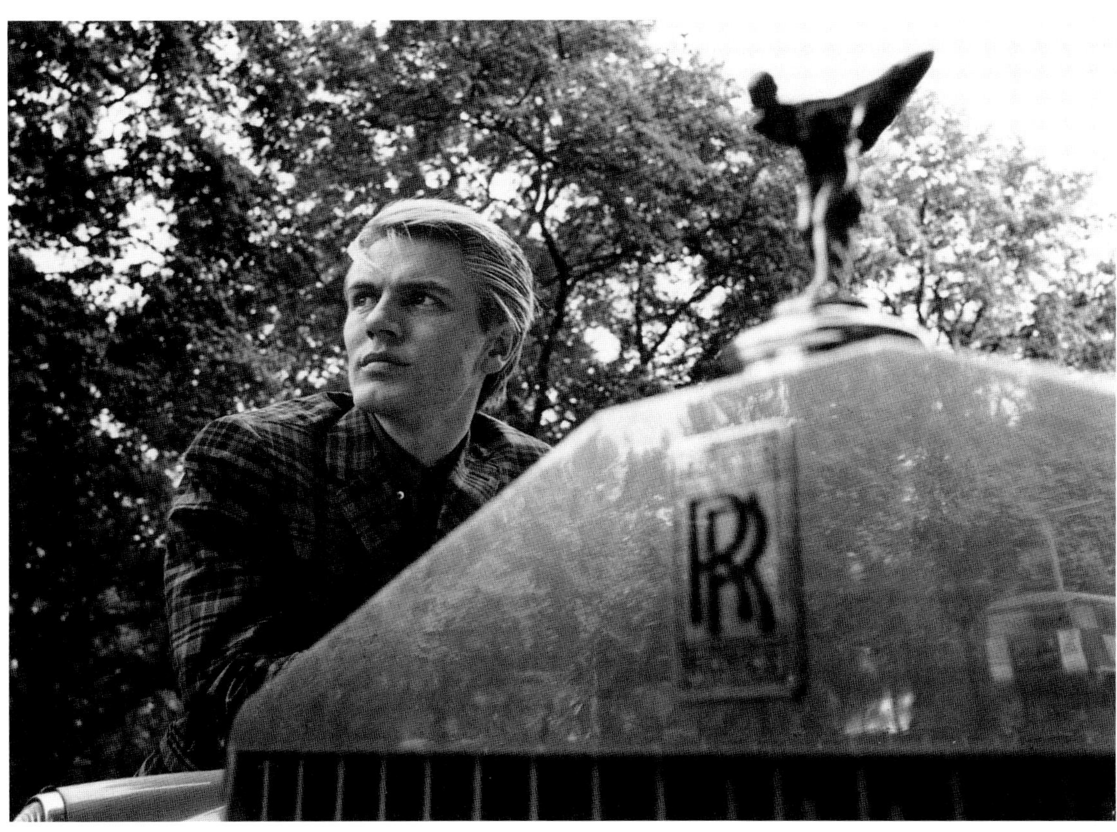

Adam Faith, early 1960s (no. 41)

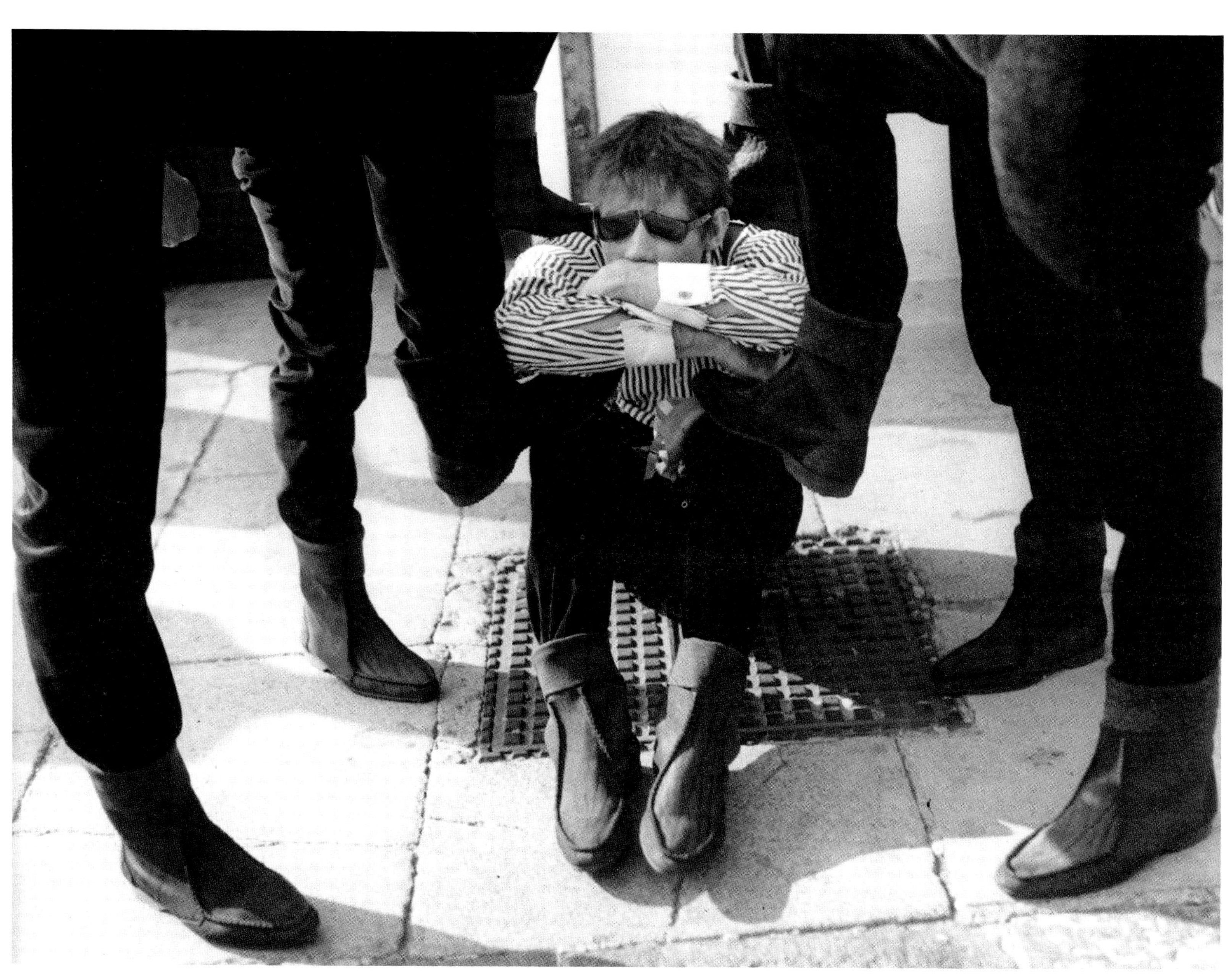

Jim Dale (as Vince Philpot) and **The Drags** (no. 42)

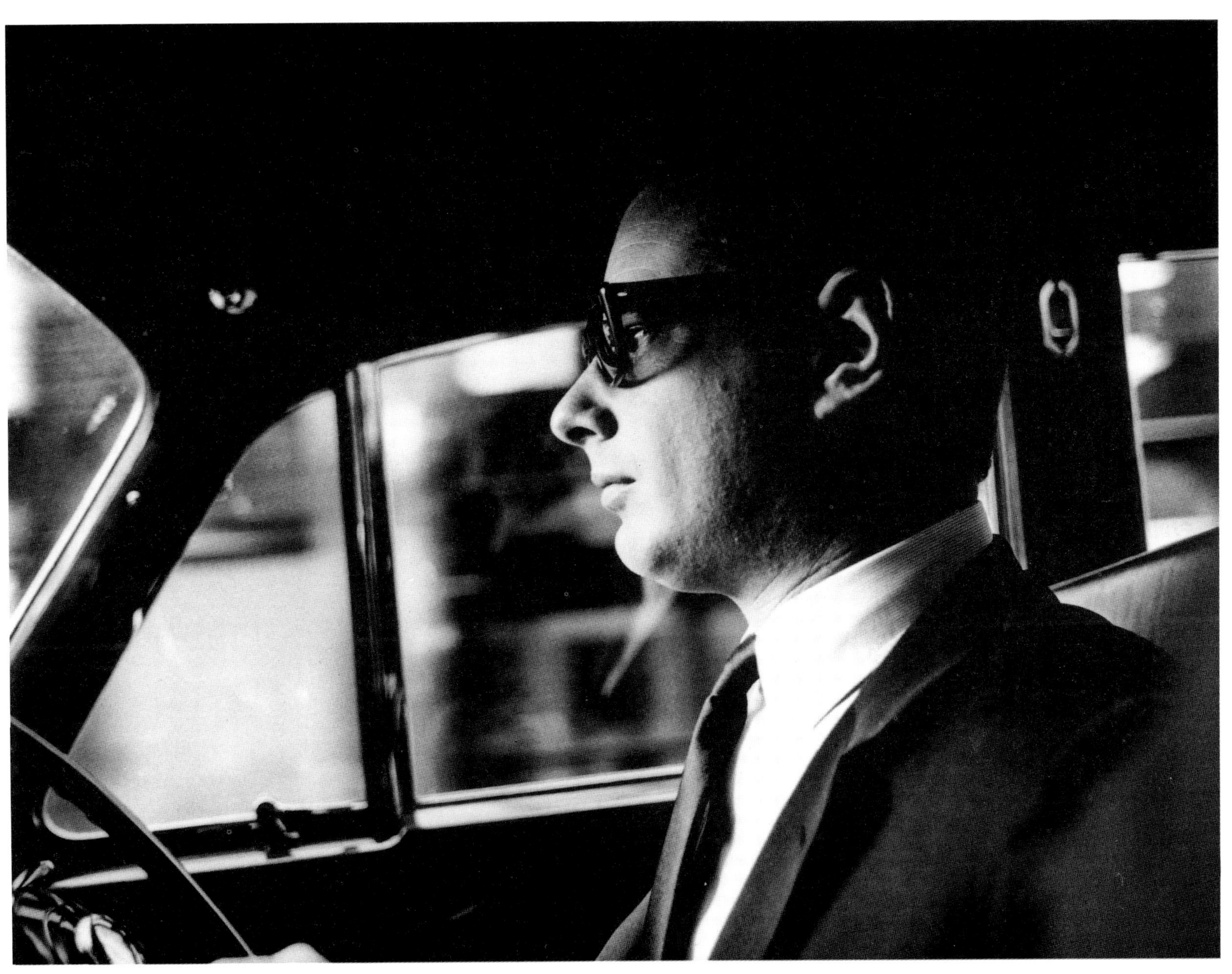

Brian Epstein, 1963 (no. 43)

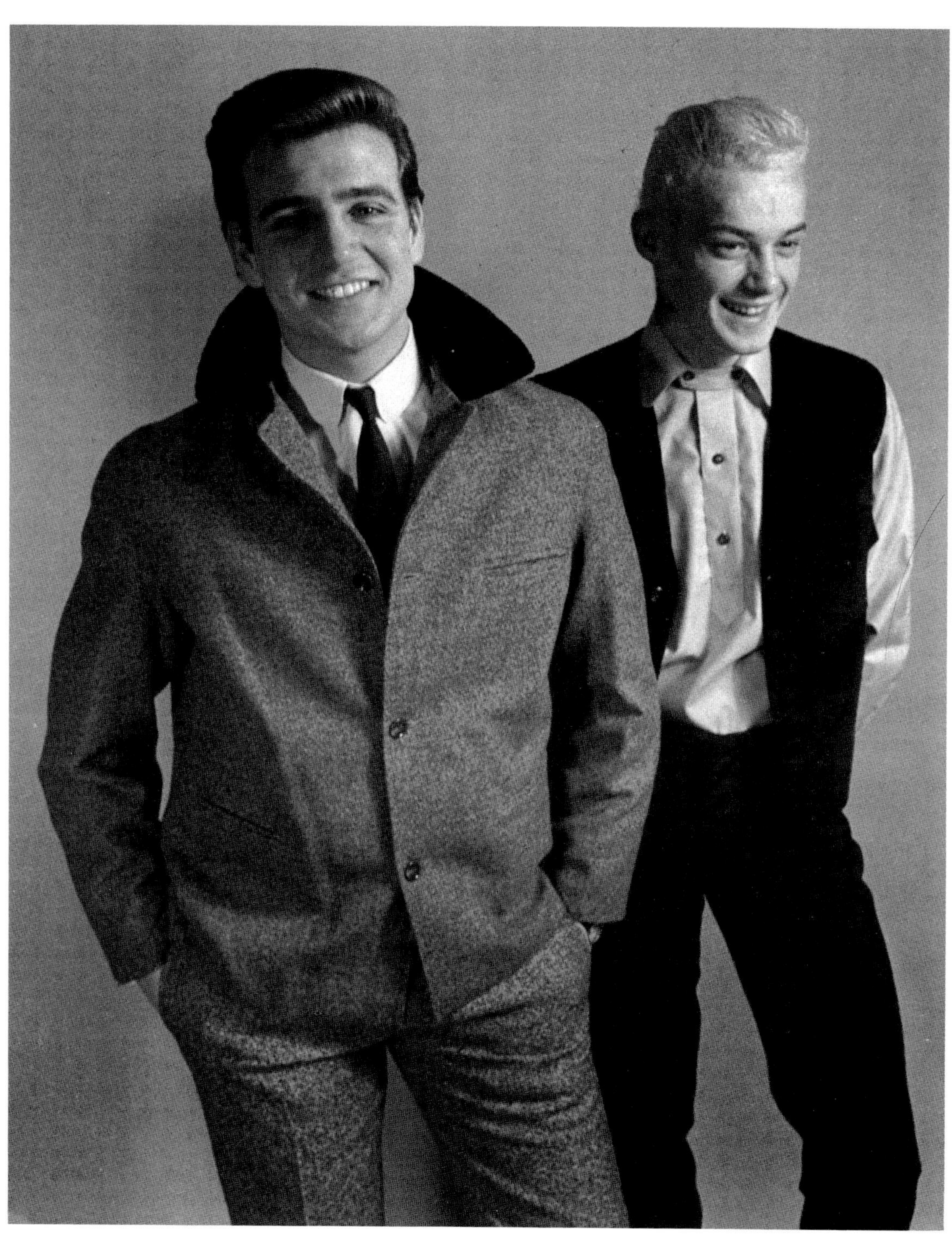

Billy J. Kramer and **Heinz**, 1963 (no. 44)

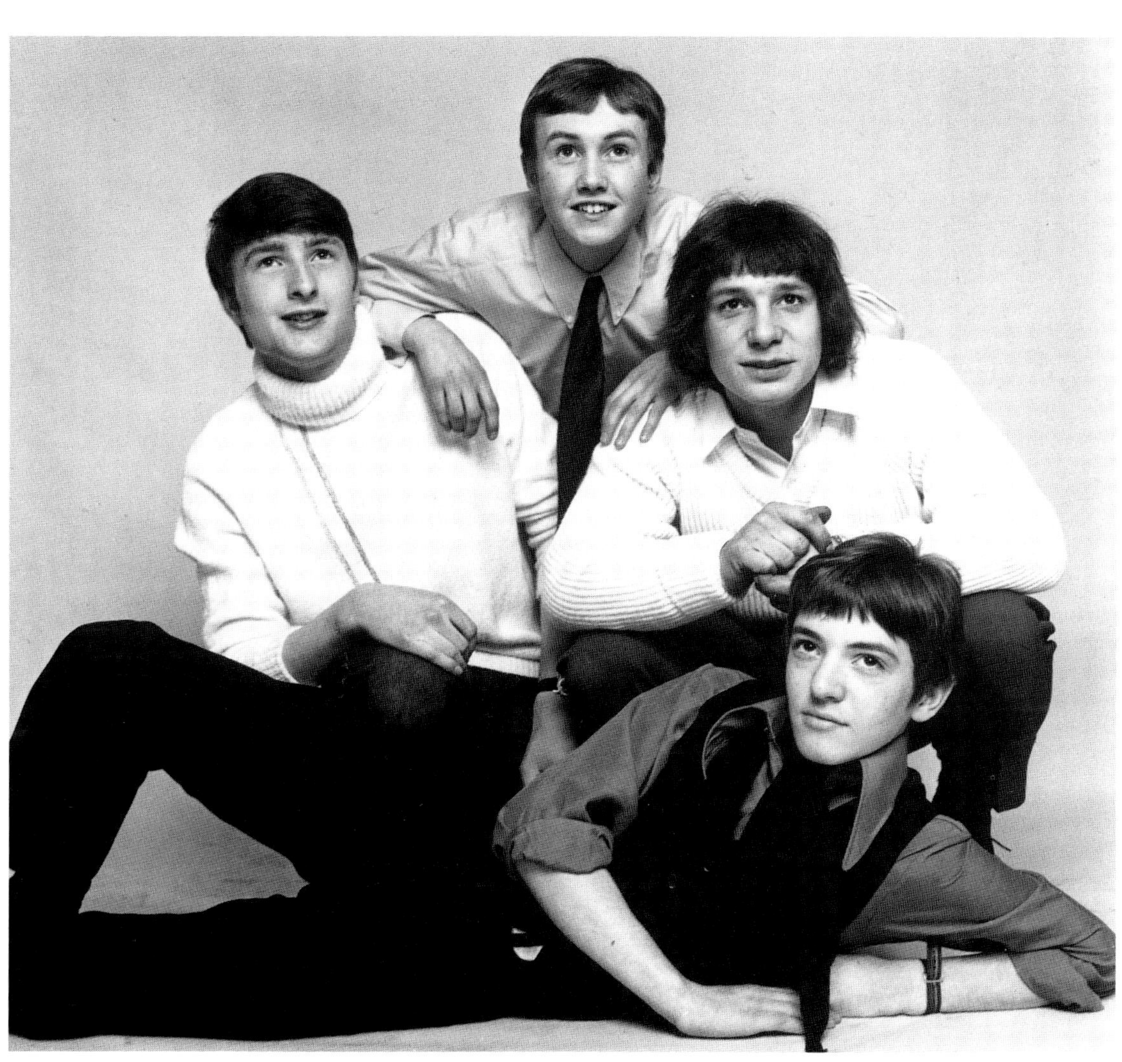

The Small Faces: Steve Marriott, Ronnie Lane, Jimmy Winston and **Kenny Jones** (no. 45)

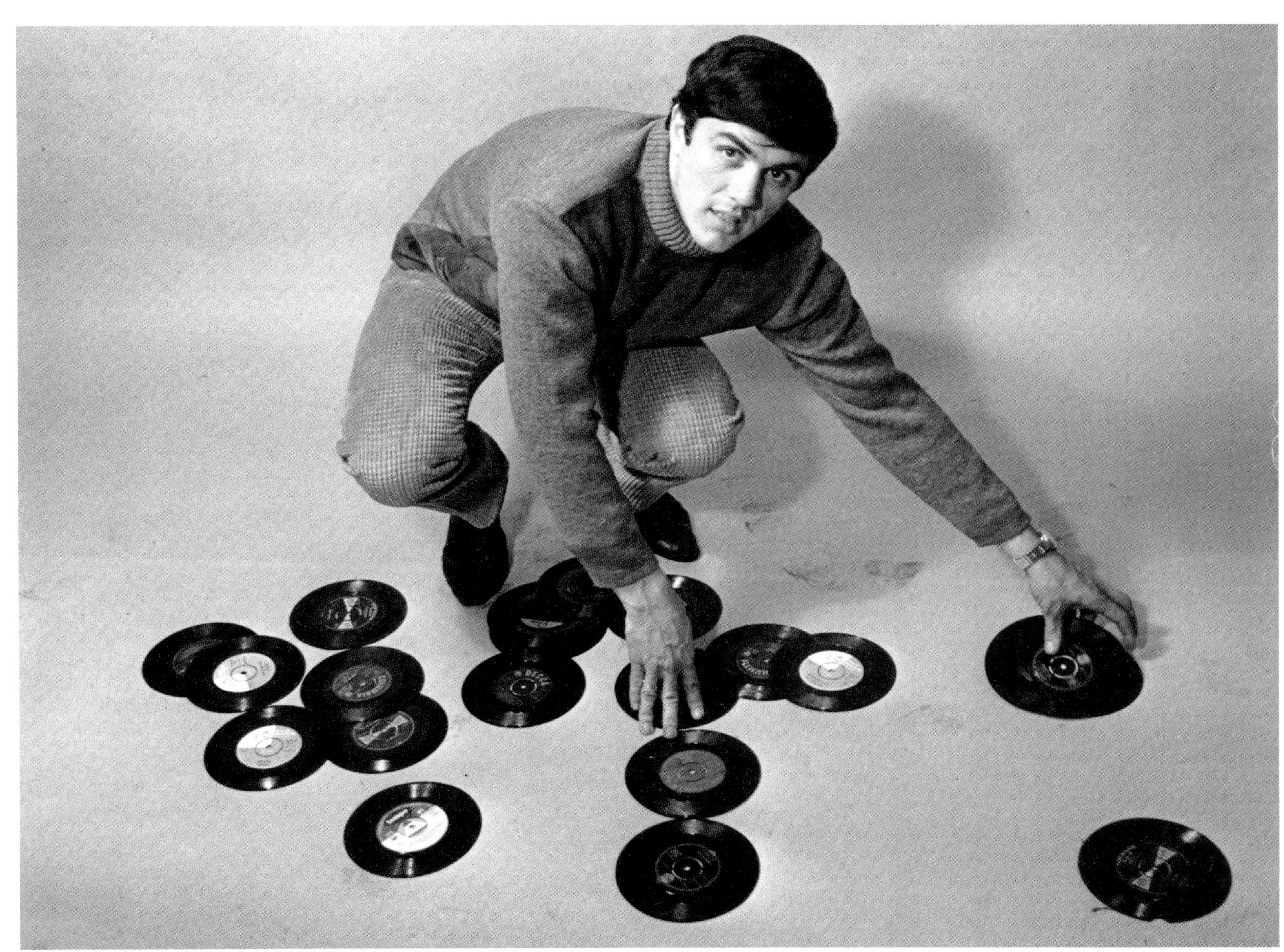

Dave Clark, 1964 (no. 47)

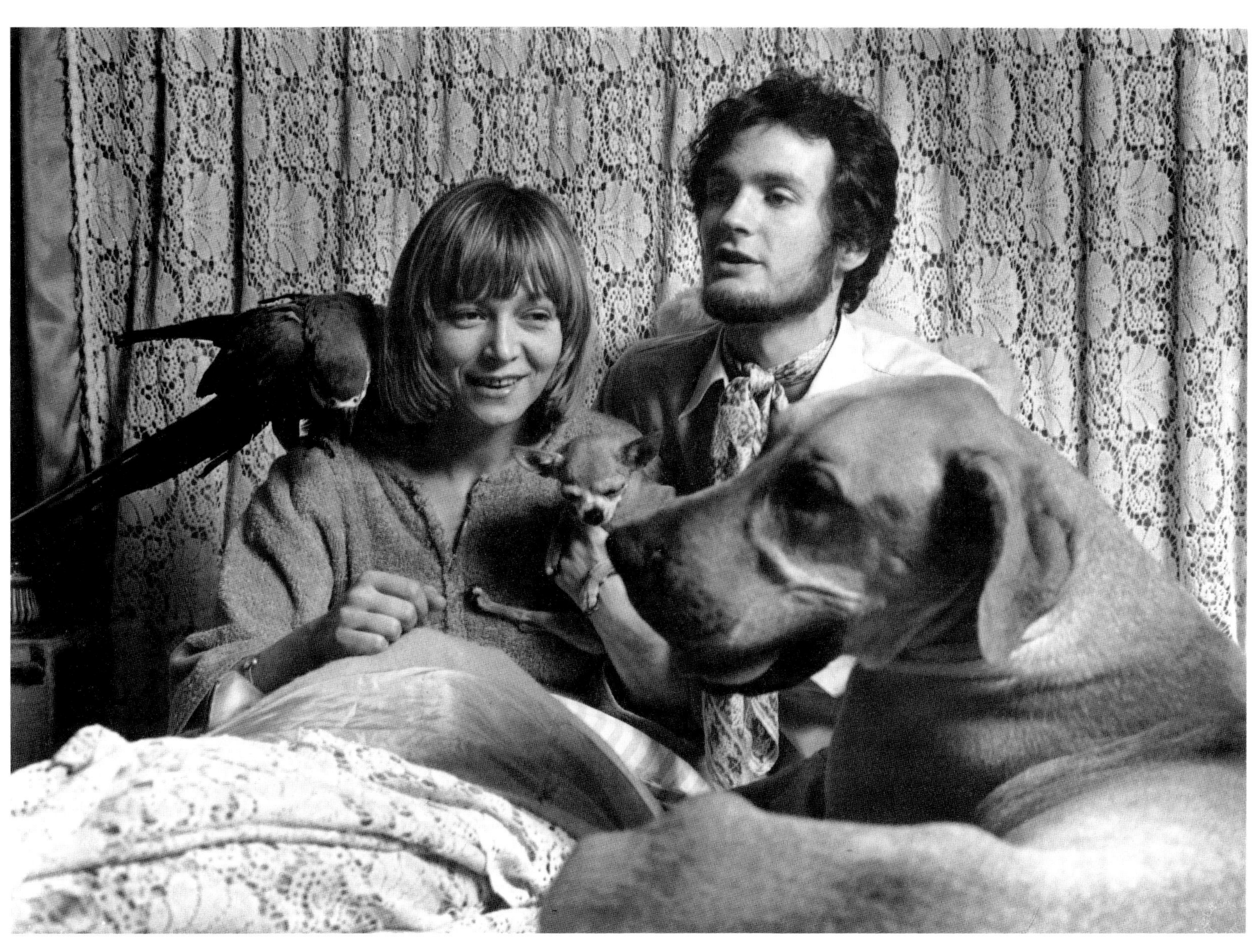

Kenny and Lee Everett, 1960s (no. 46)

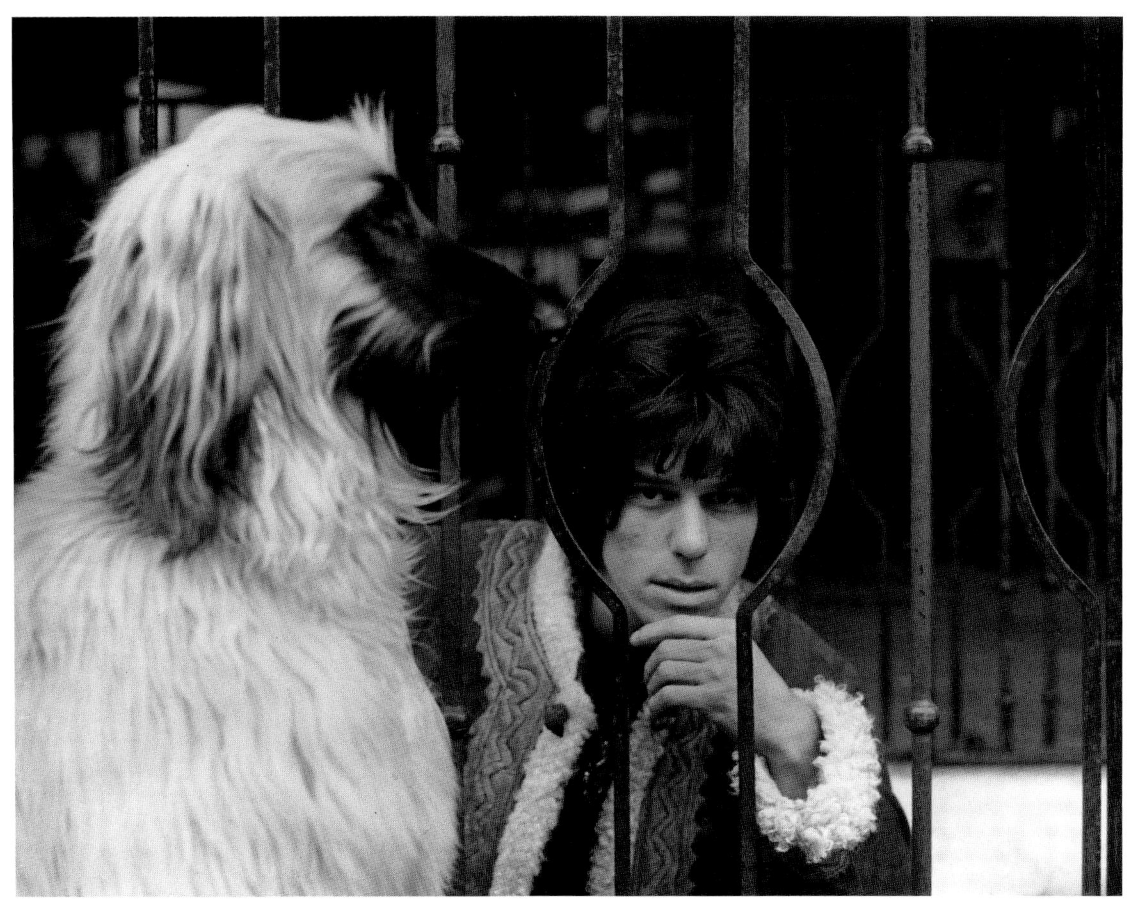

Jeff Beck with Afghan hound, 1967 (no. 54)

Donovan, 1965 (no. 55)

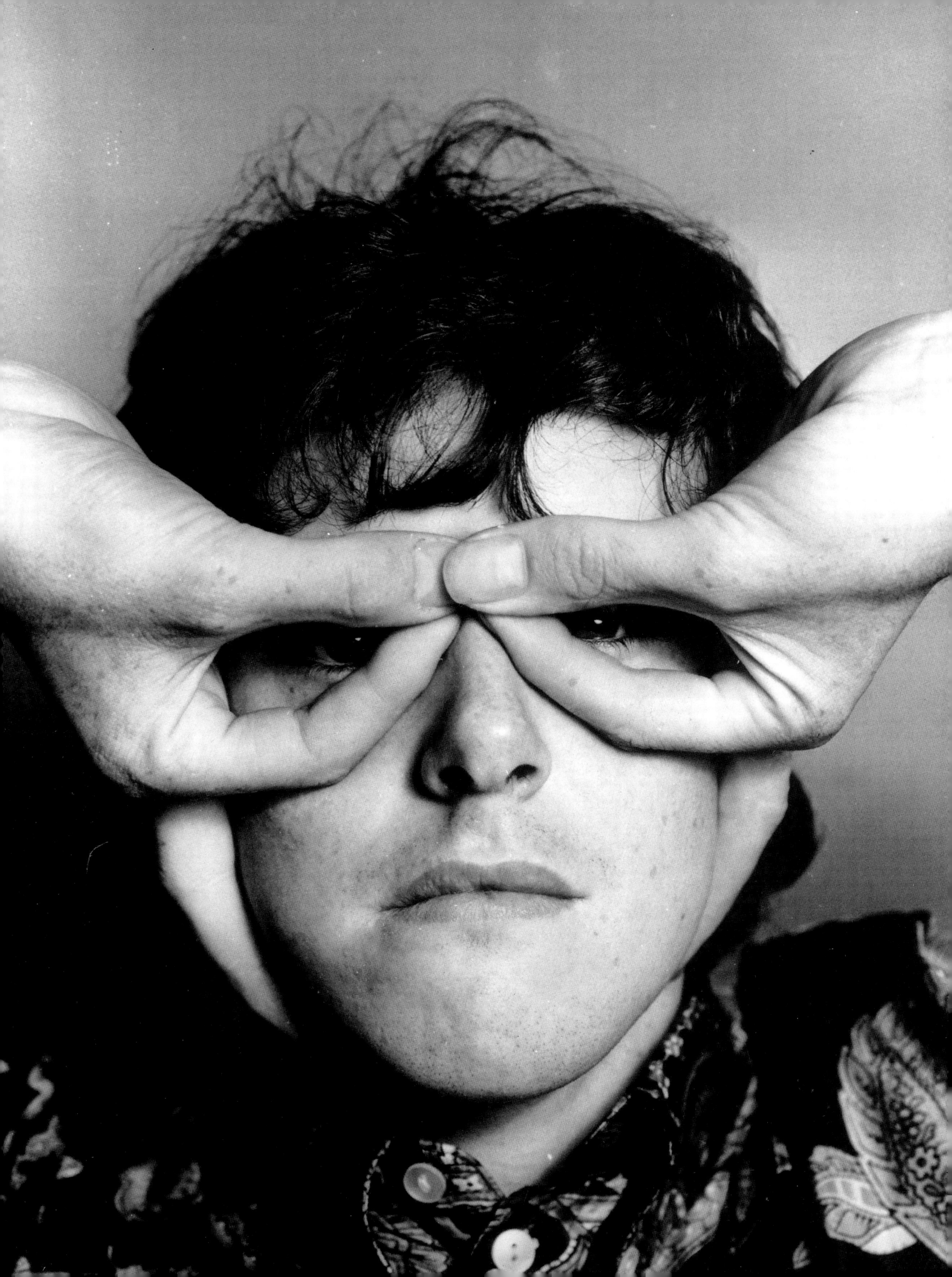

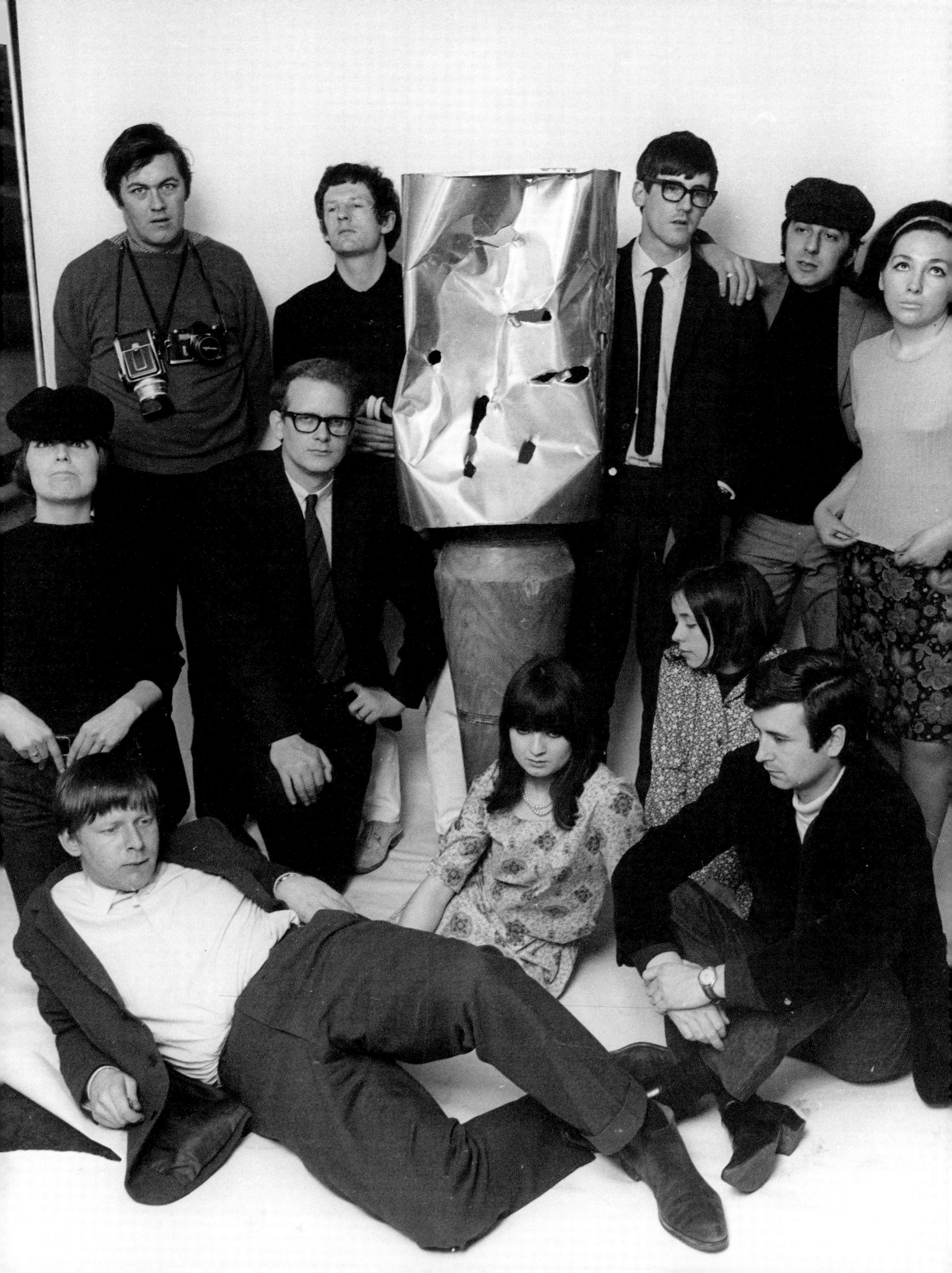

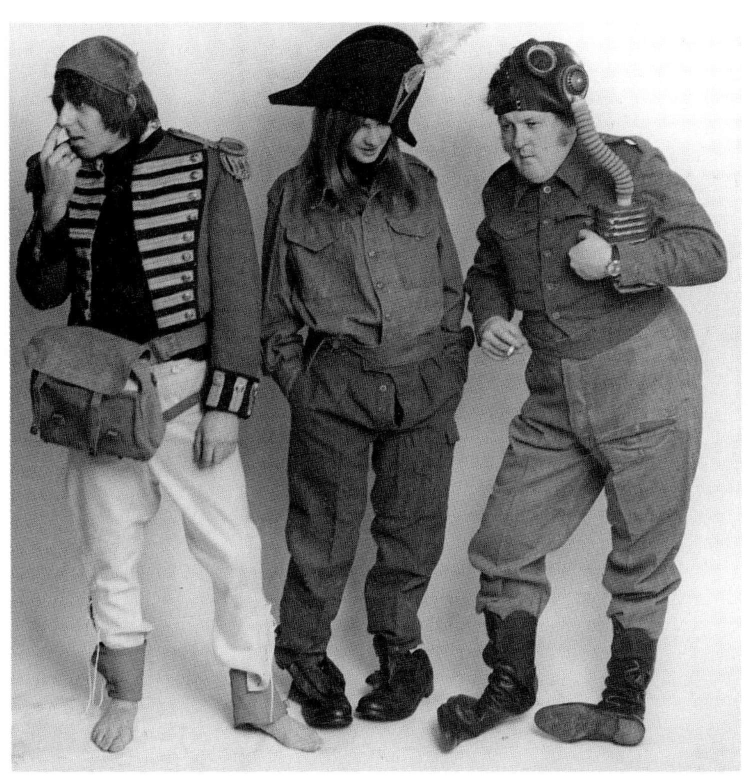

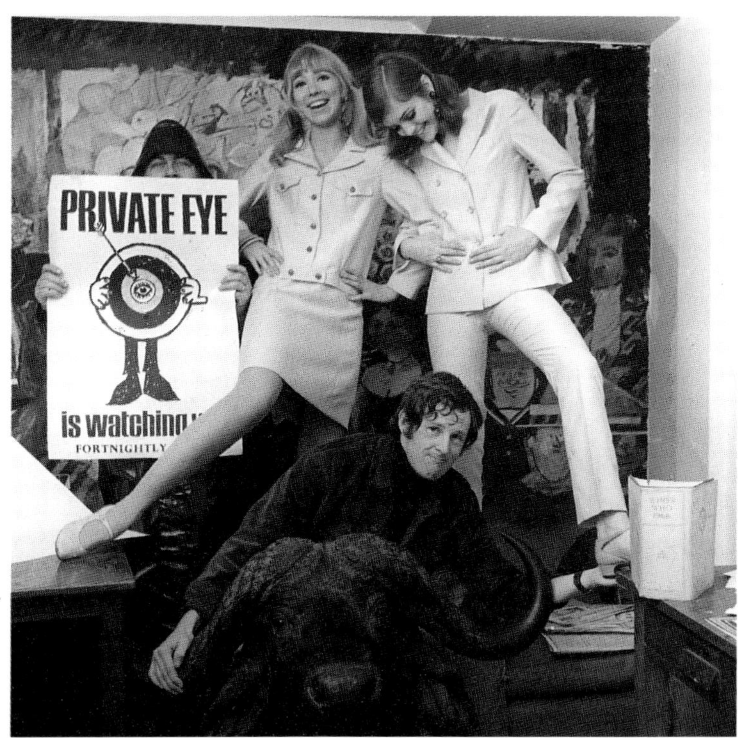

Private Eye group: left to right, back row: **Richard Ingrams, Tony Rushton, Paul Foot, Barry Fantoni, Jill Brooke**; middle row: **Gabby Hughes, Peter Usborne, unknown, Jan Elson, Michael Wale**; foreground: **John Wells**, 1965 (no. 72)

Private Eye Fashion, 1967 (no. 75)

Richard Ingrams and **Tony Rushton**, 1966 (no. 73)

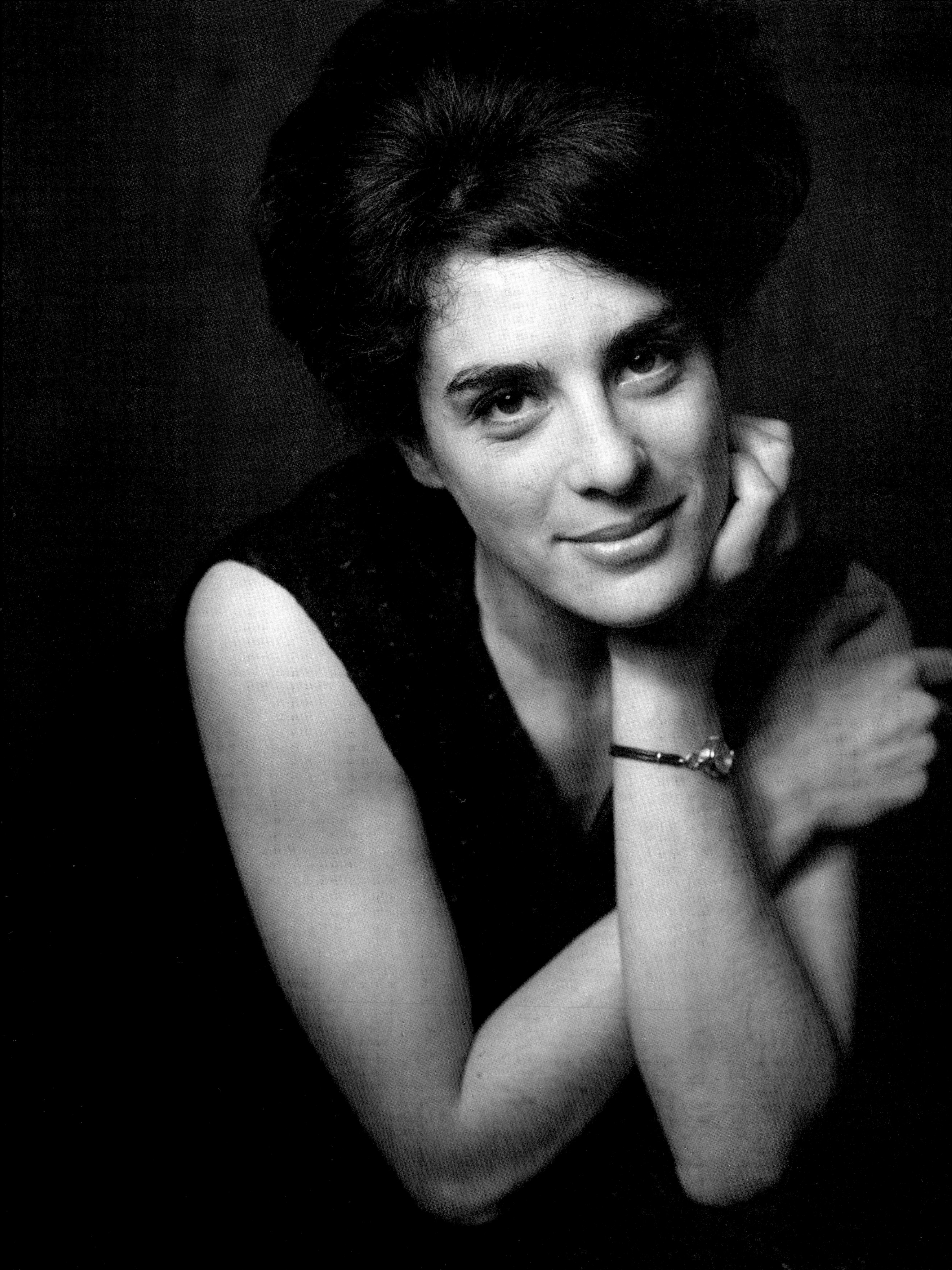

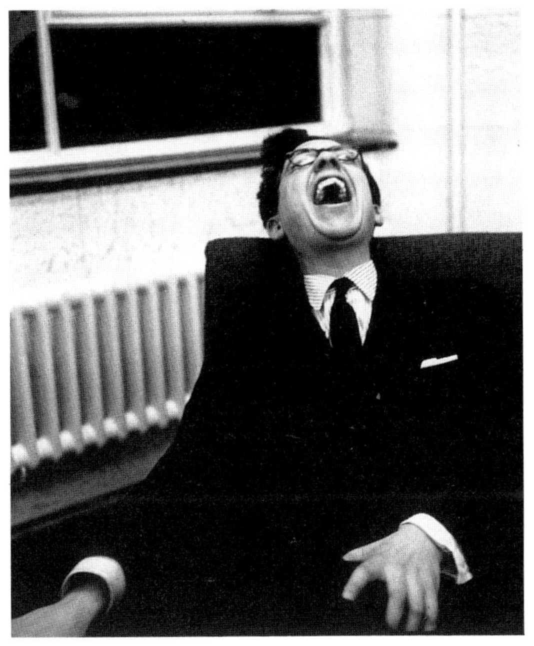

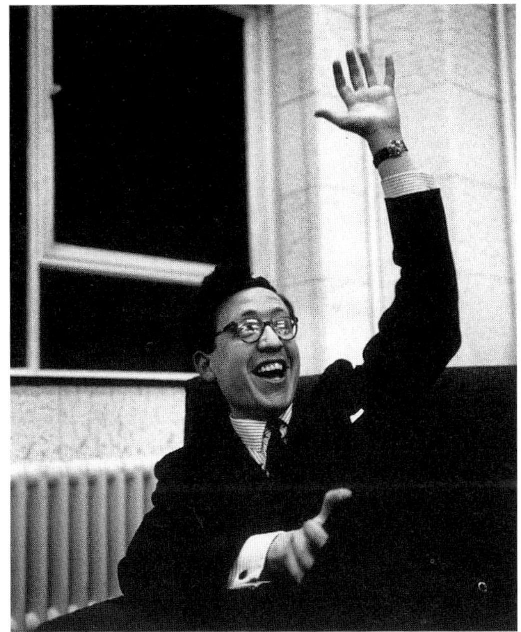

Eleanor Bron, 1963 (no. 67)

Bernard Levin, 1963 (nos. 68, 69)

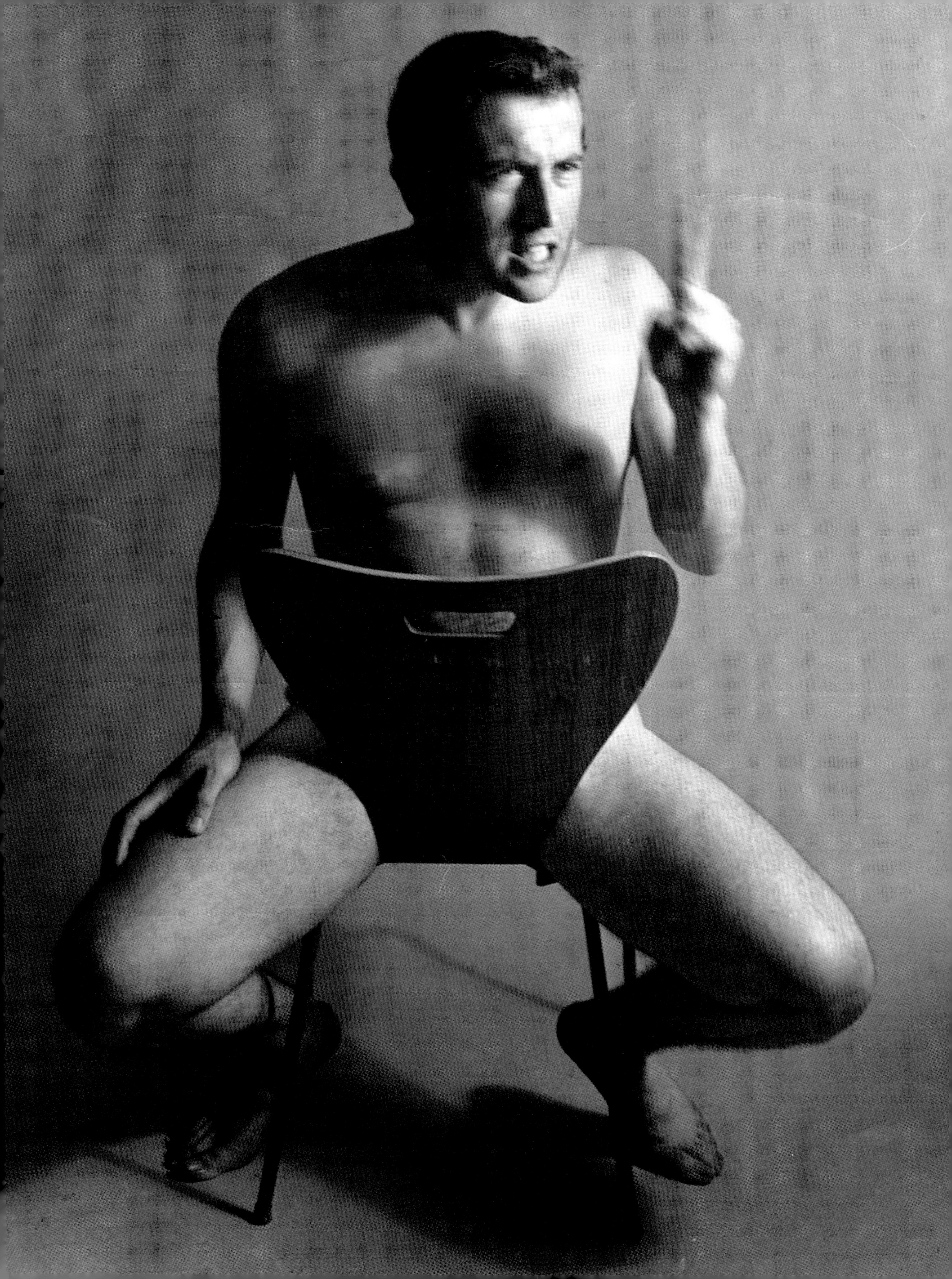

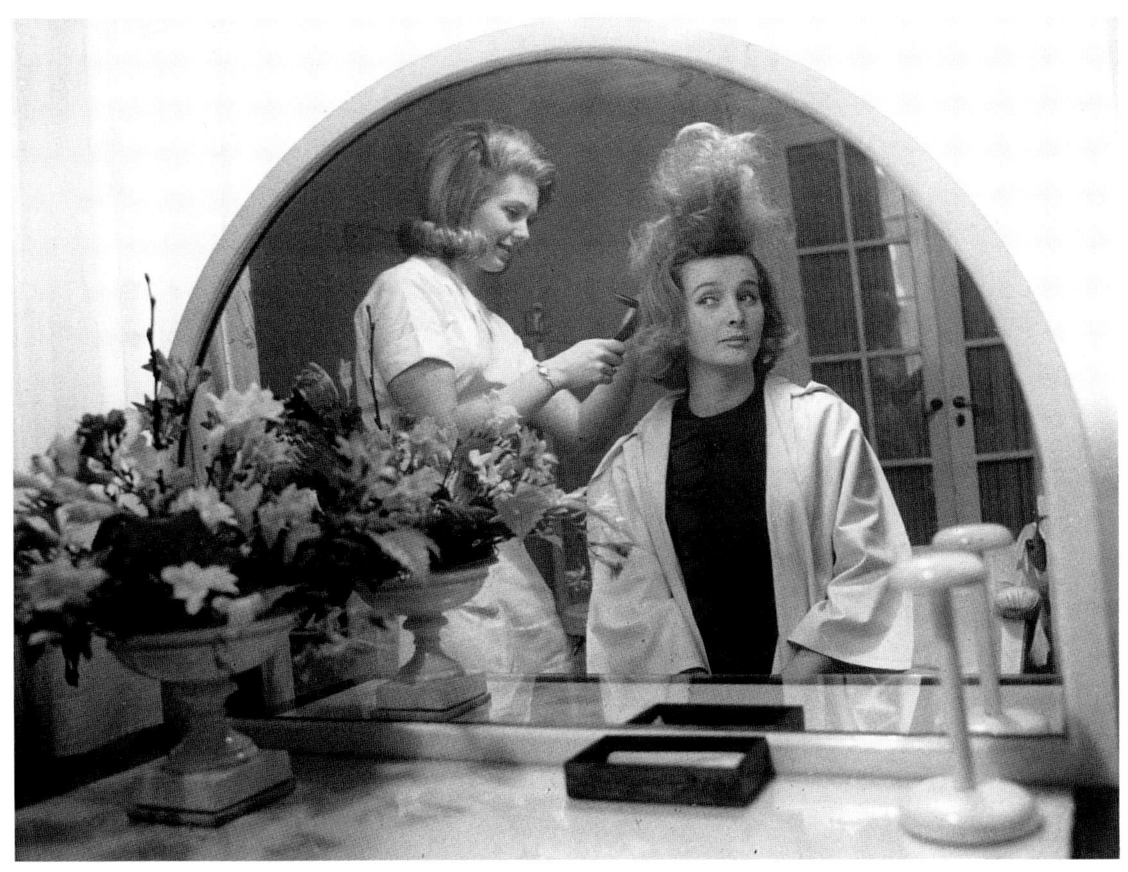

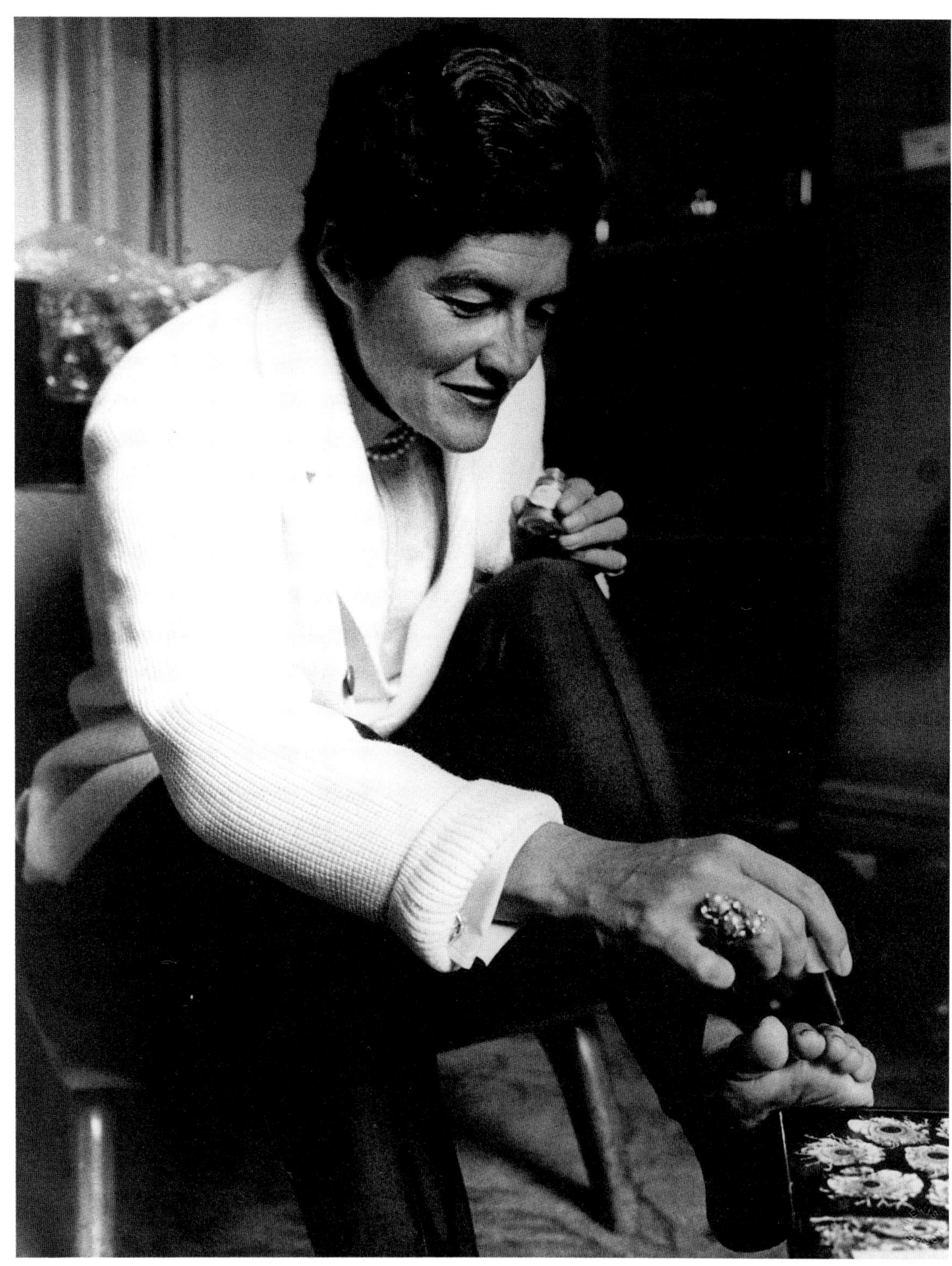

Nancy Spain, early 1960s (no. 34)

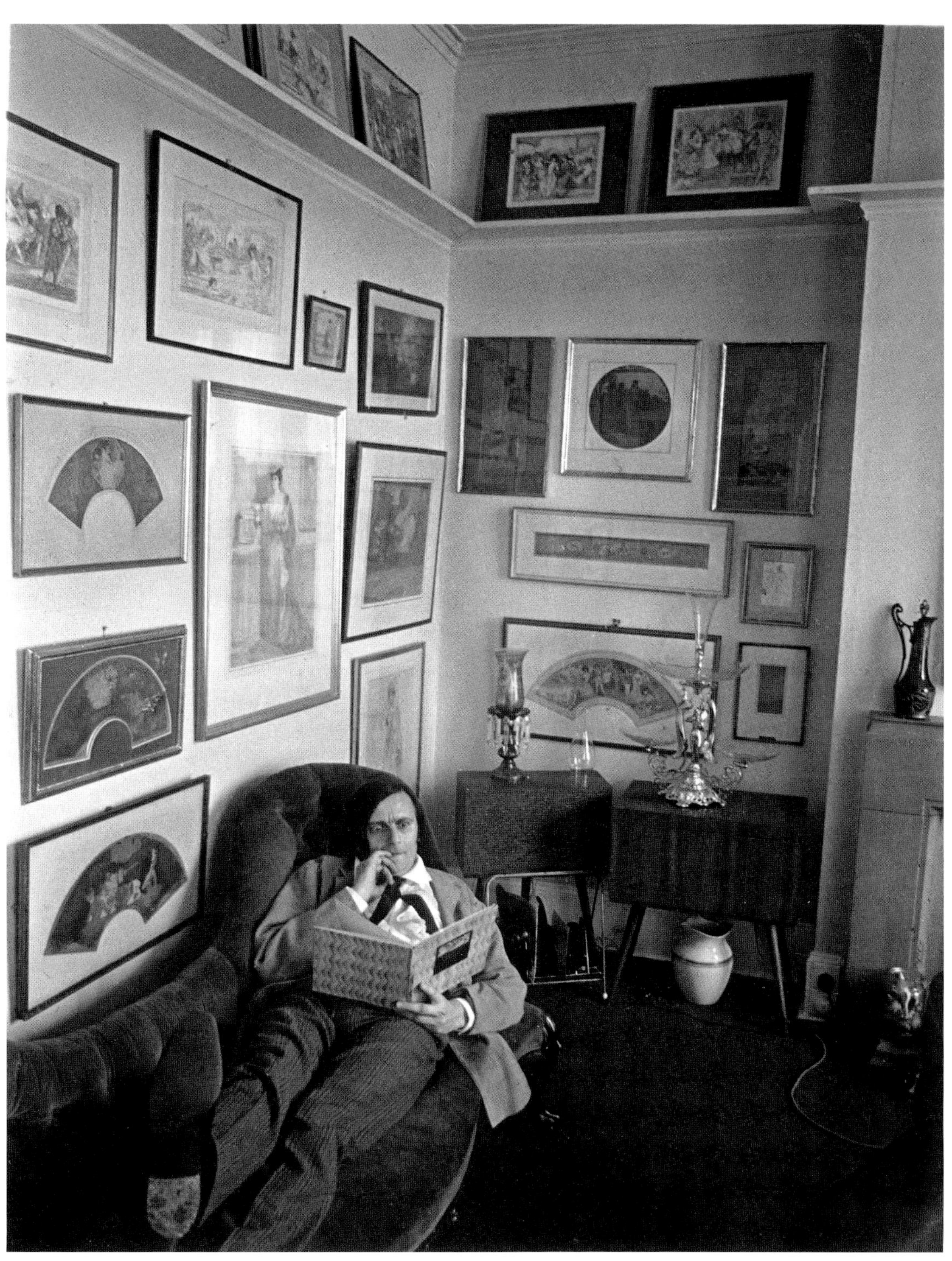

Barry Humphries, 1962 (no. 65)

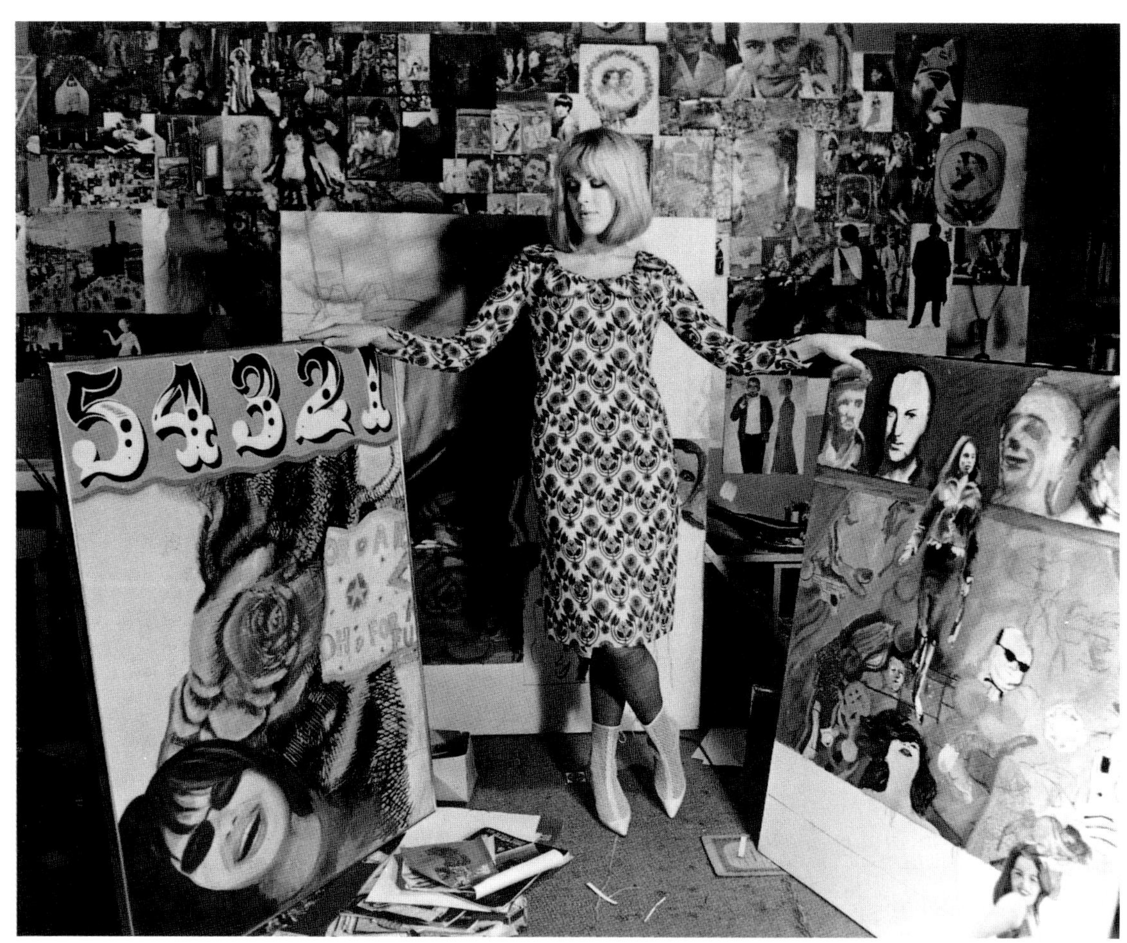

Pauline Boty, 1963 (no. 48)

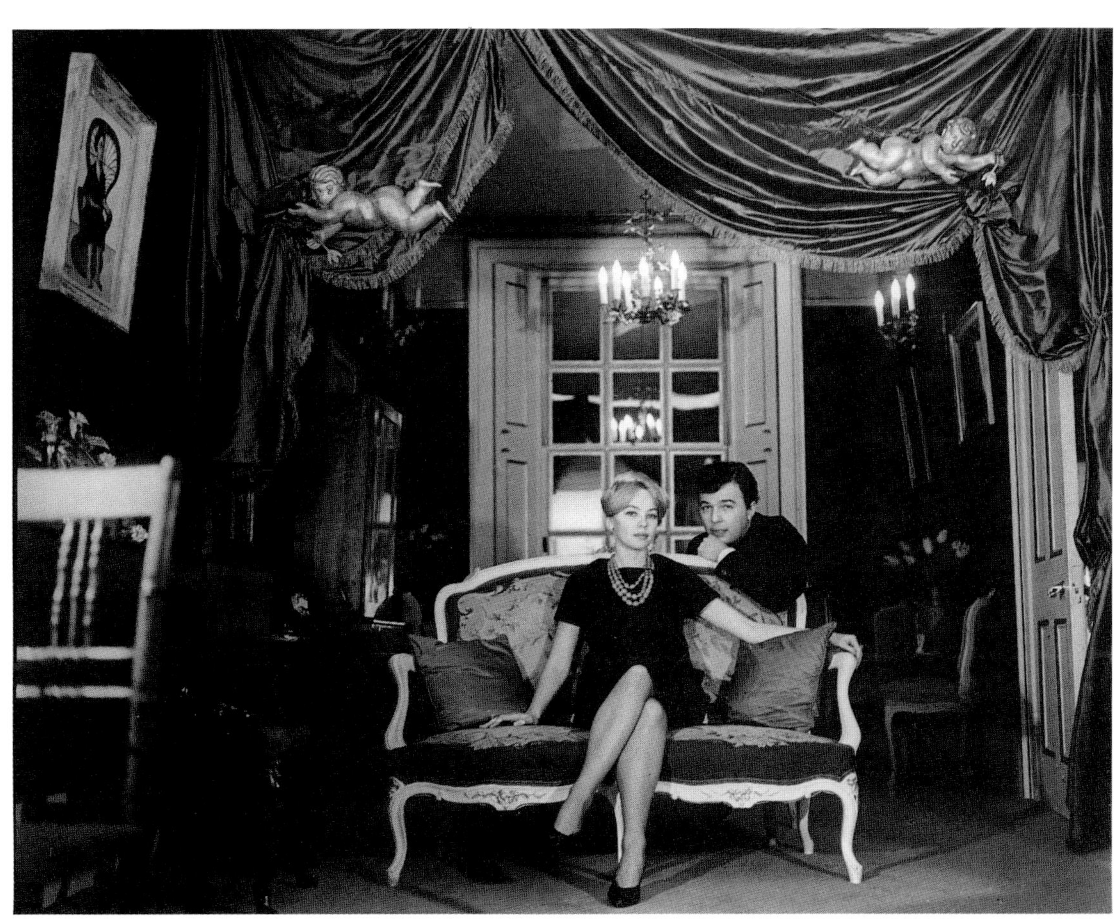

Peter Hall and **Leslie Caron**, 1961 (no. 17)

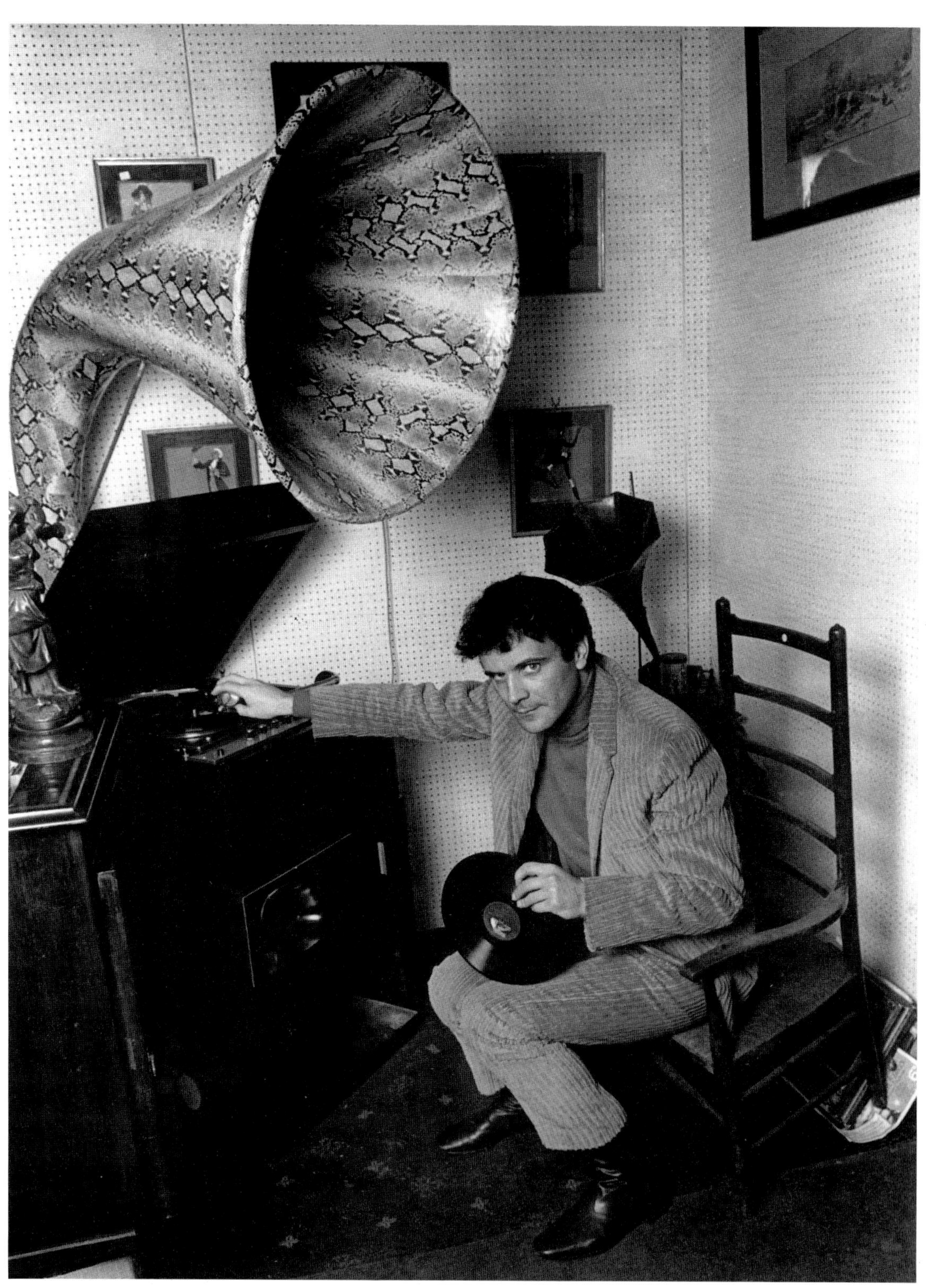

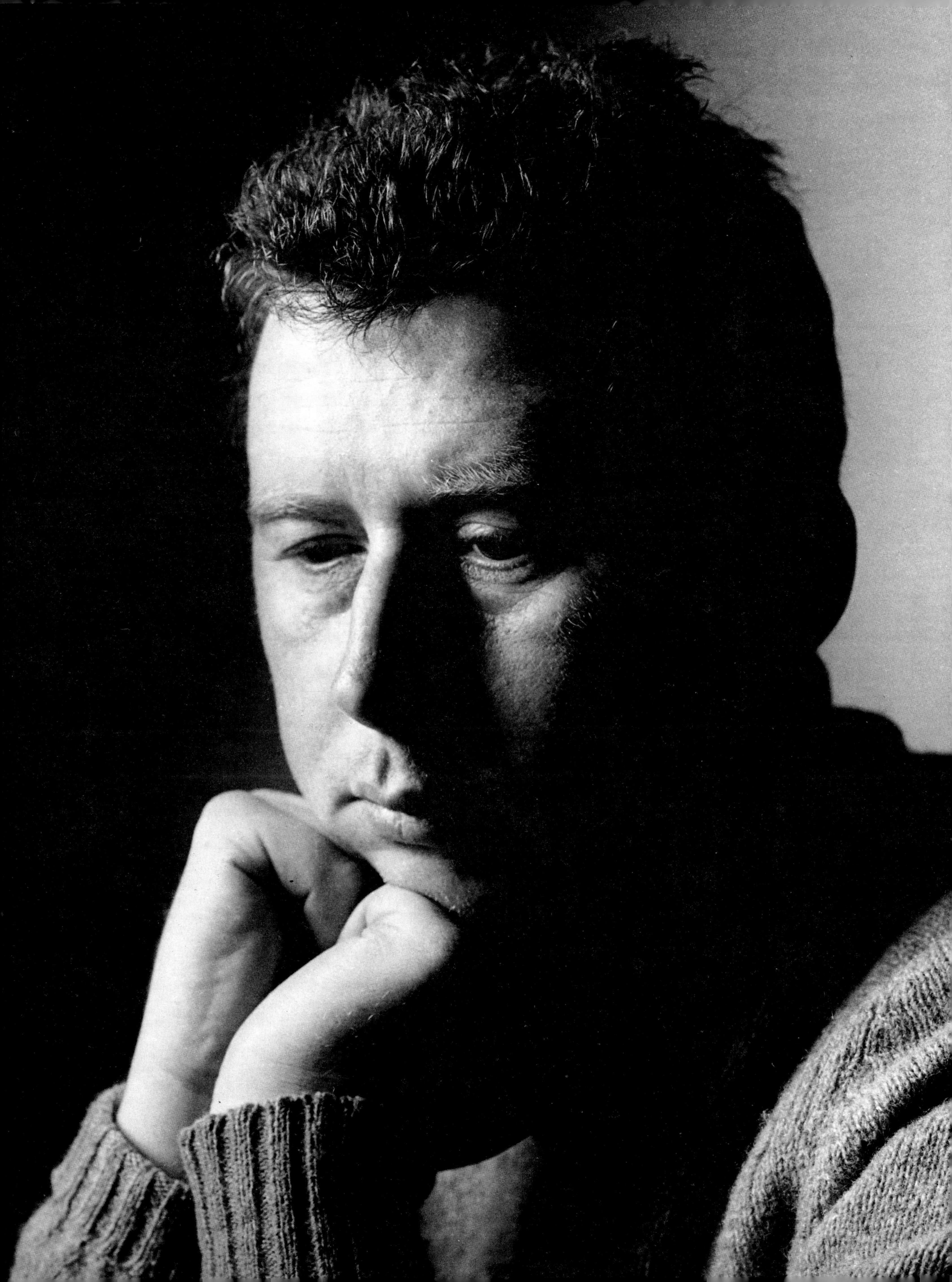

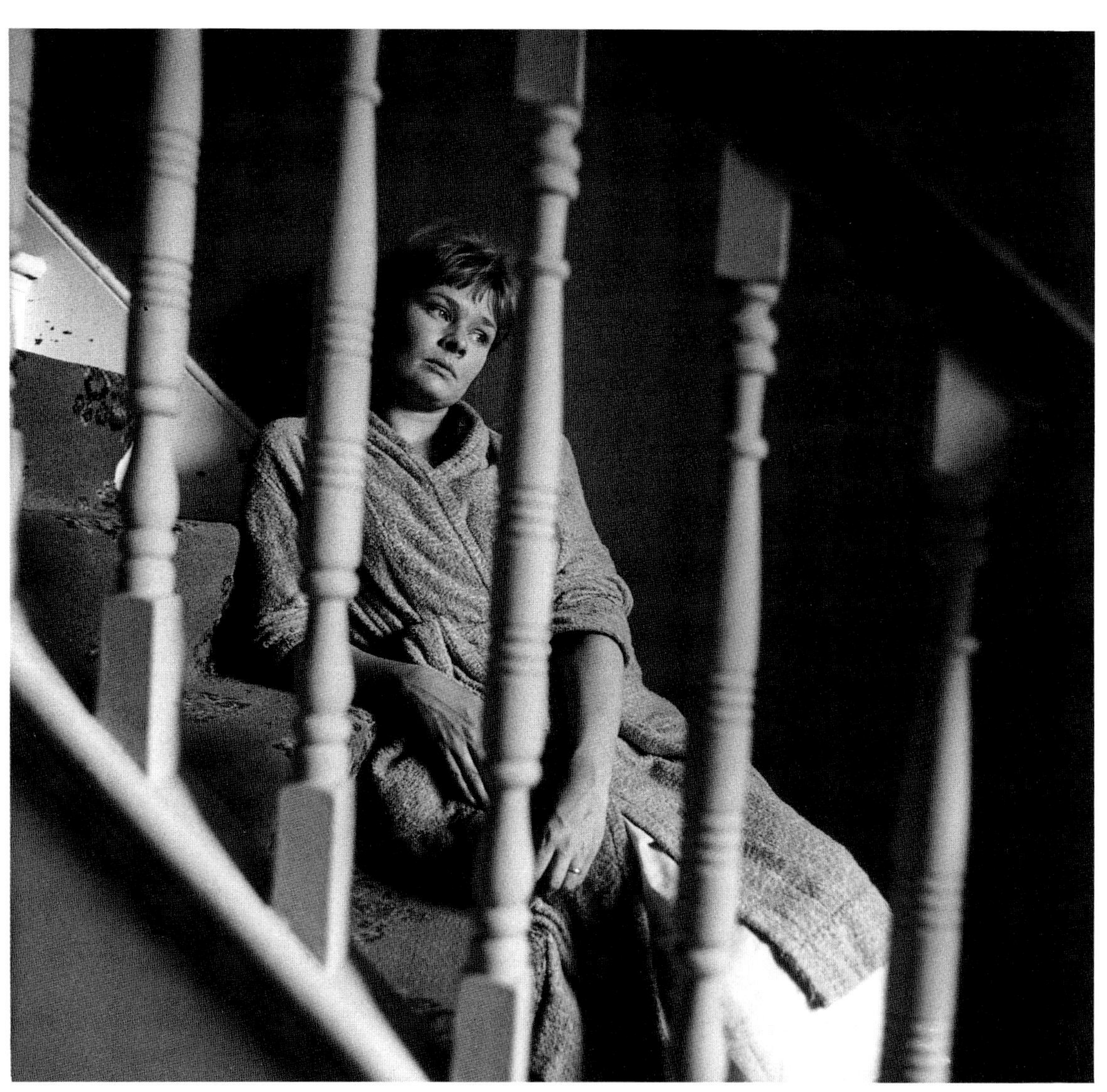

Judi Dench, 1965 (no. 28)

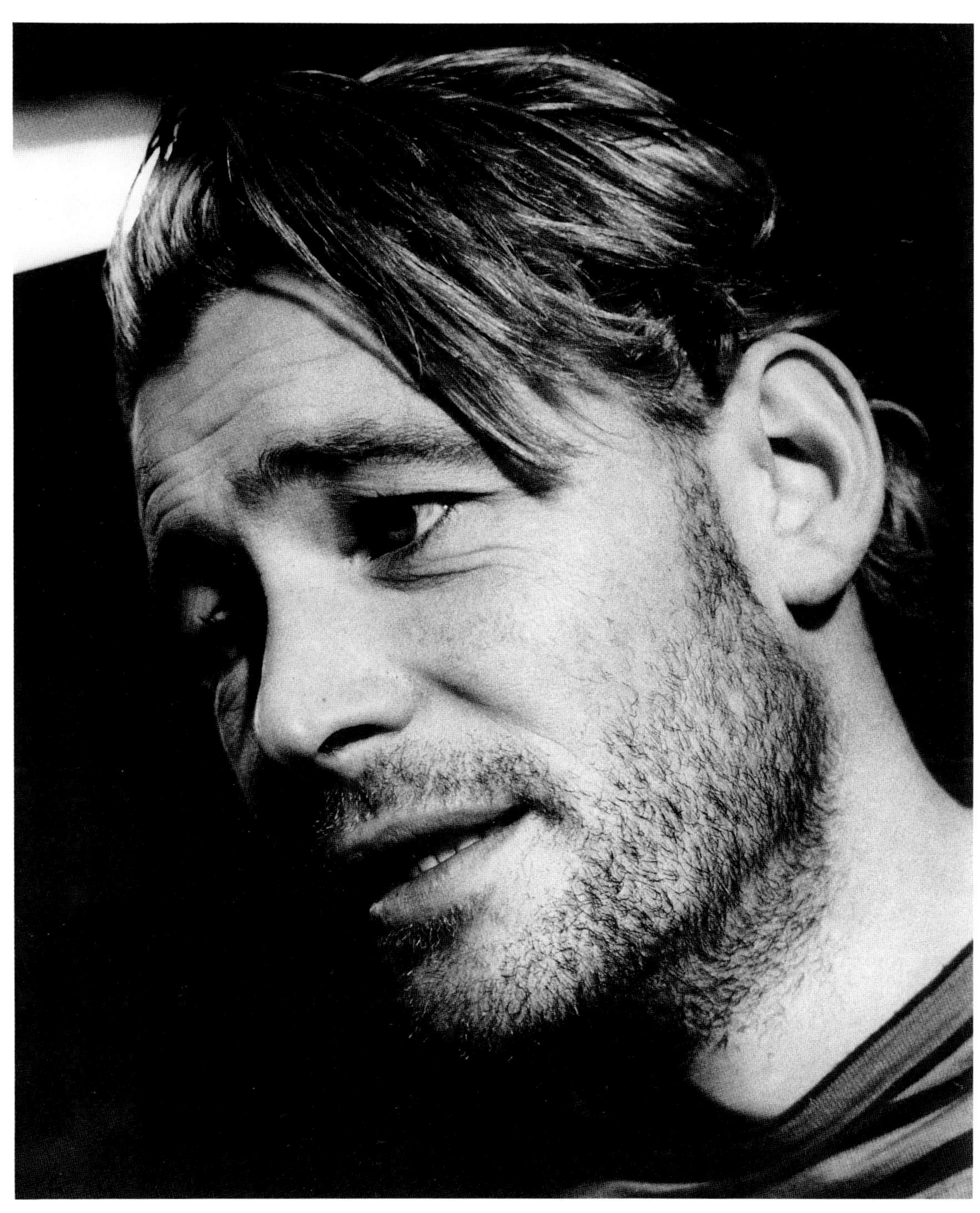

Peter O'Toole, 1963 (no. 29)

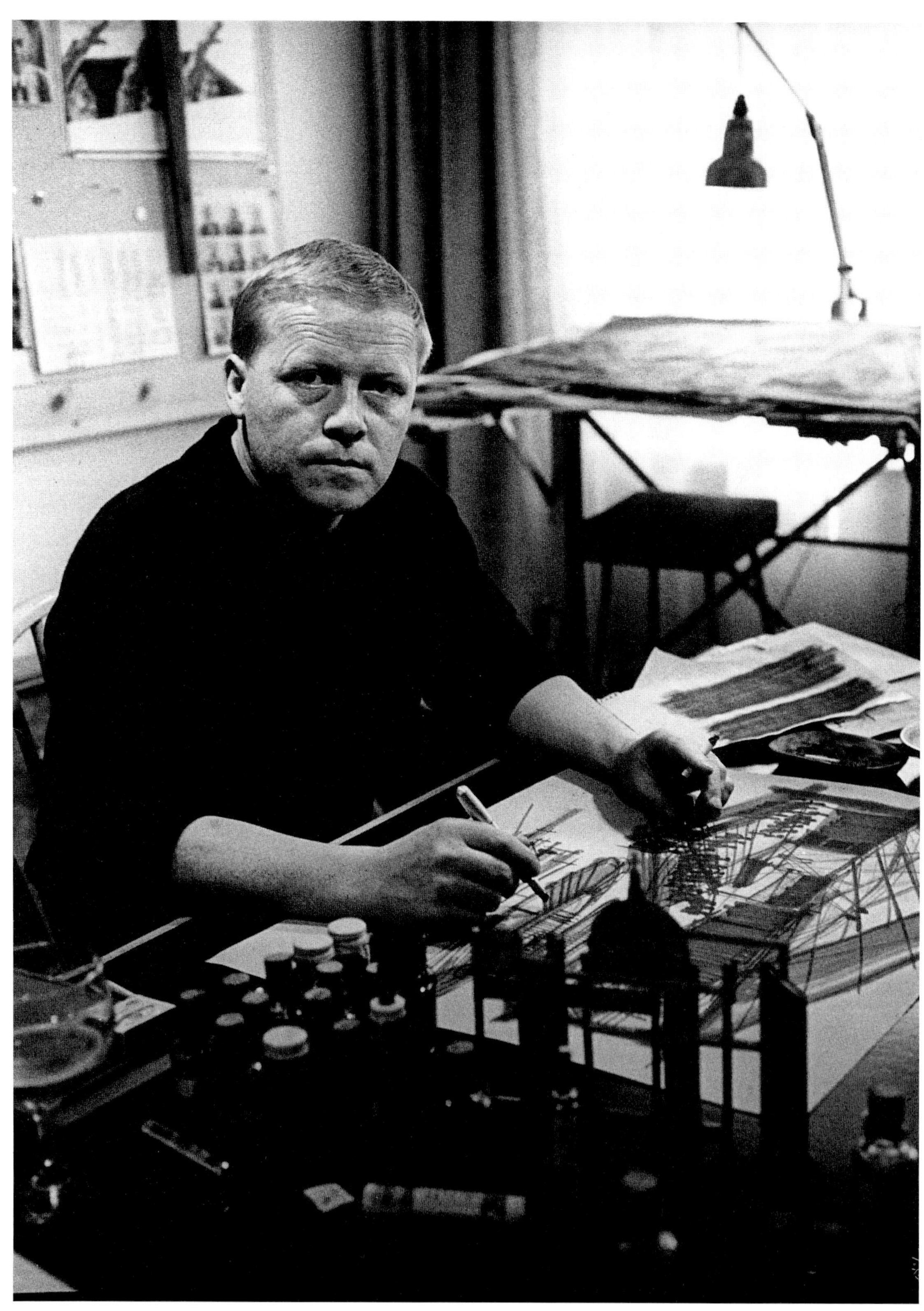

Sean Kenny, 1963 (no. 32)

James Wedge, early 1960s (no. 33)

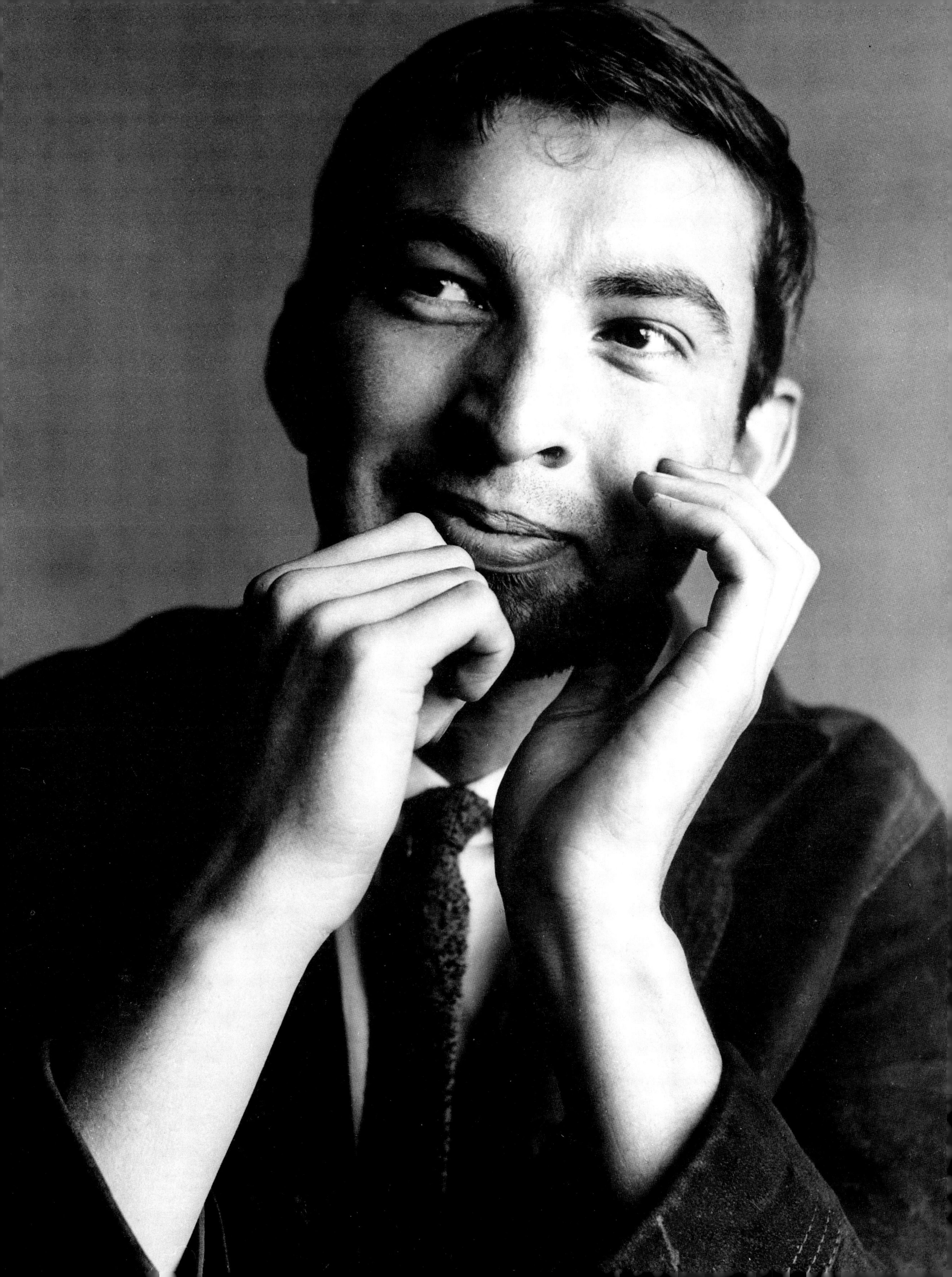

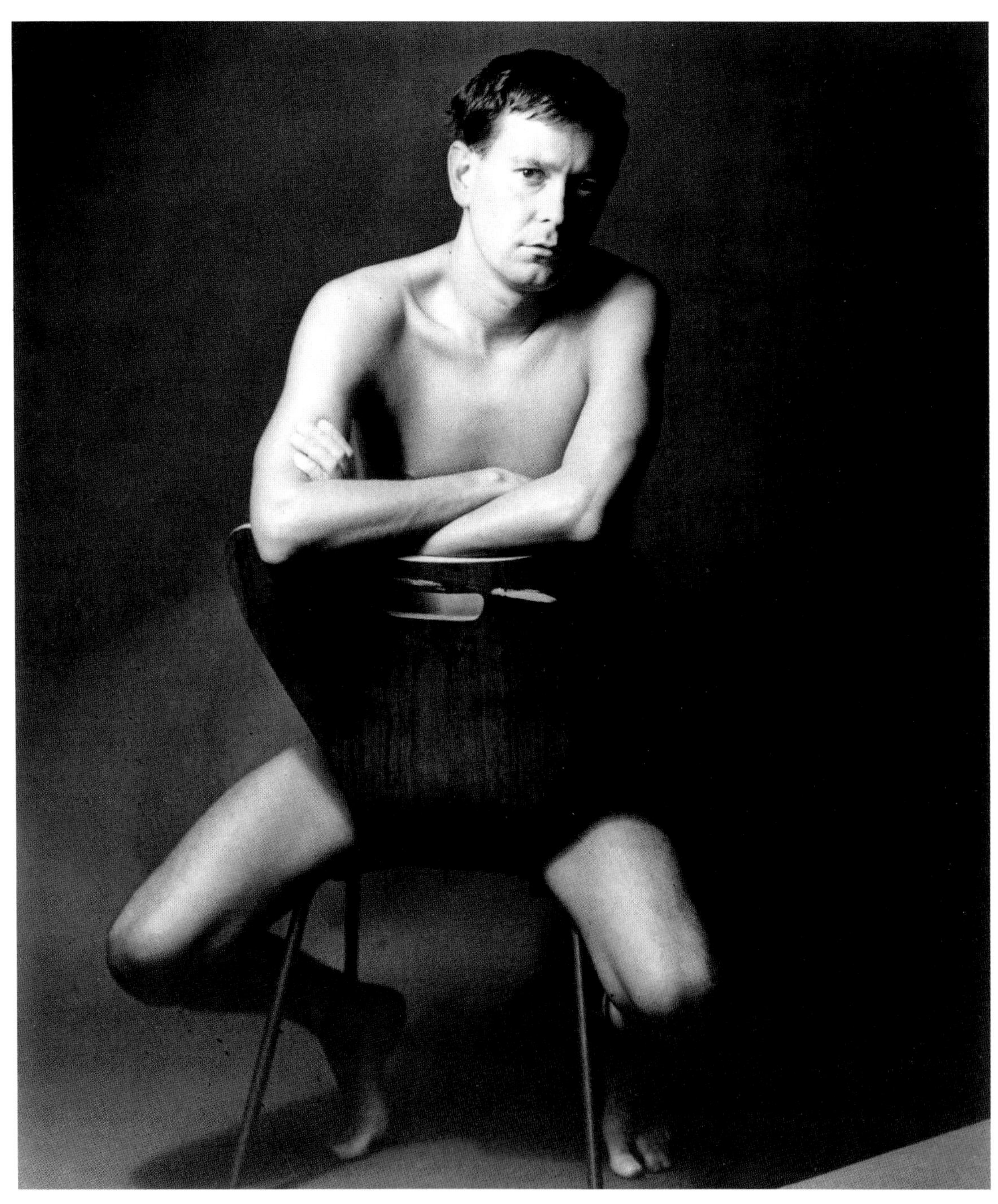

Joe Orton, 1965 (no. 91)

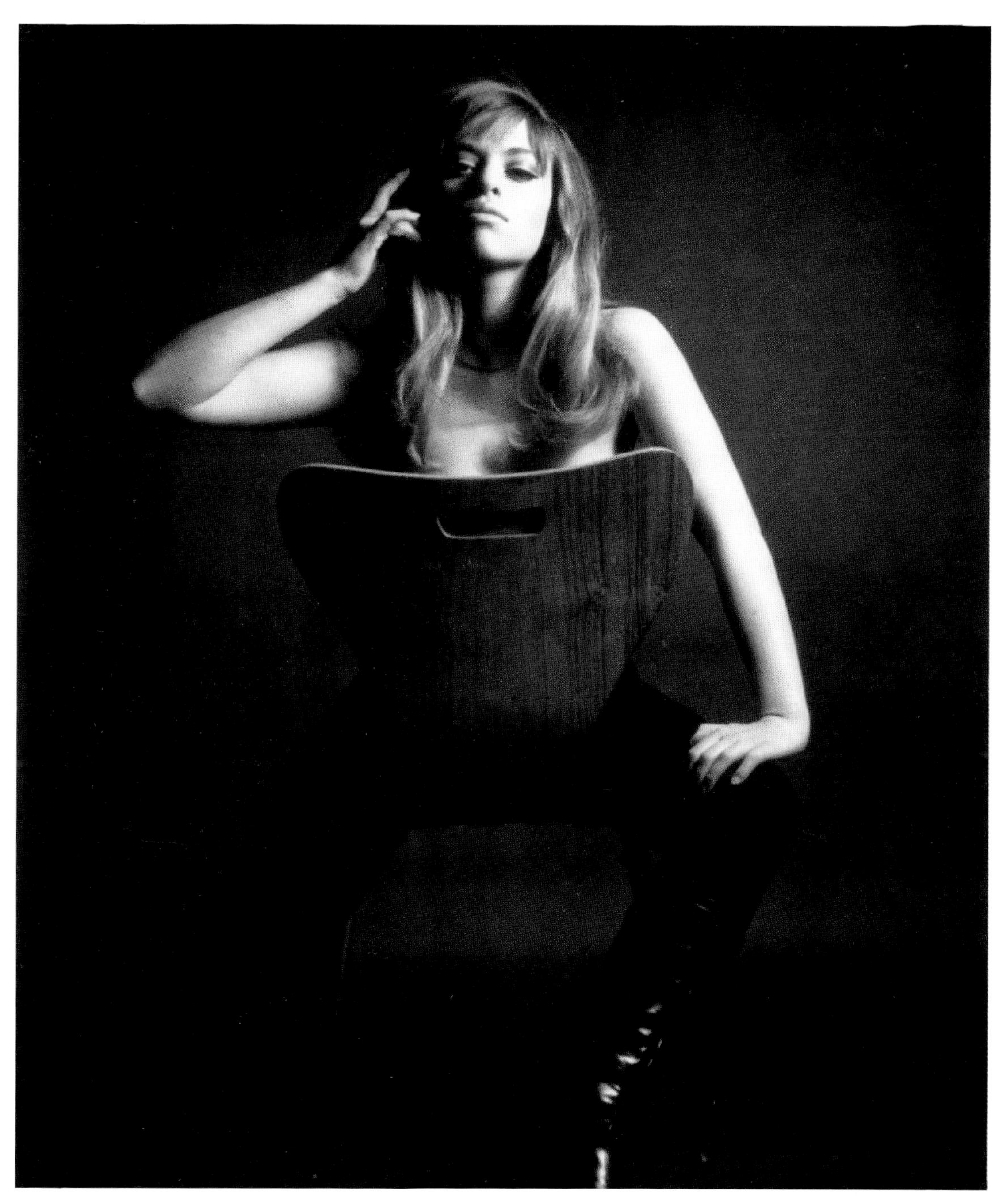

Edina Ronay, 1963 (no. 35)

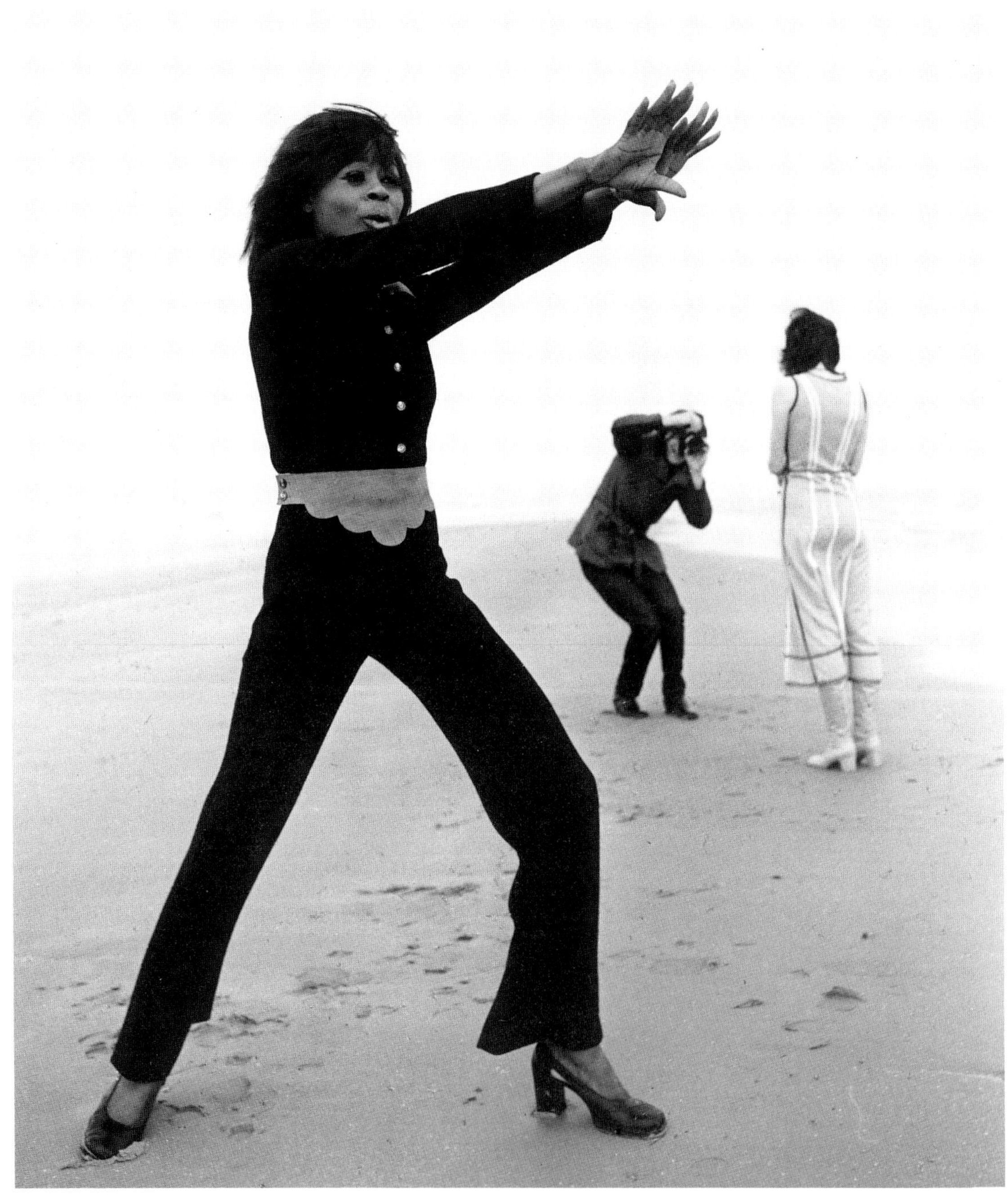

Mynah Bird and **Peter Smith** (no. 81)

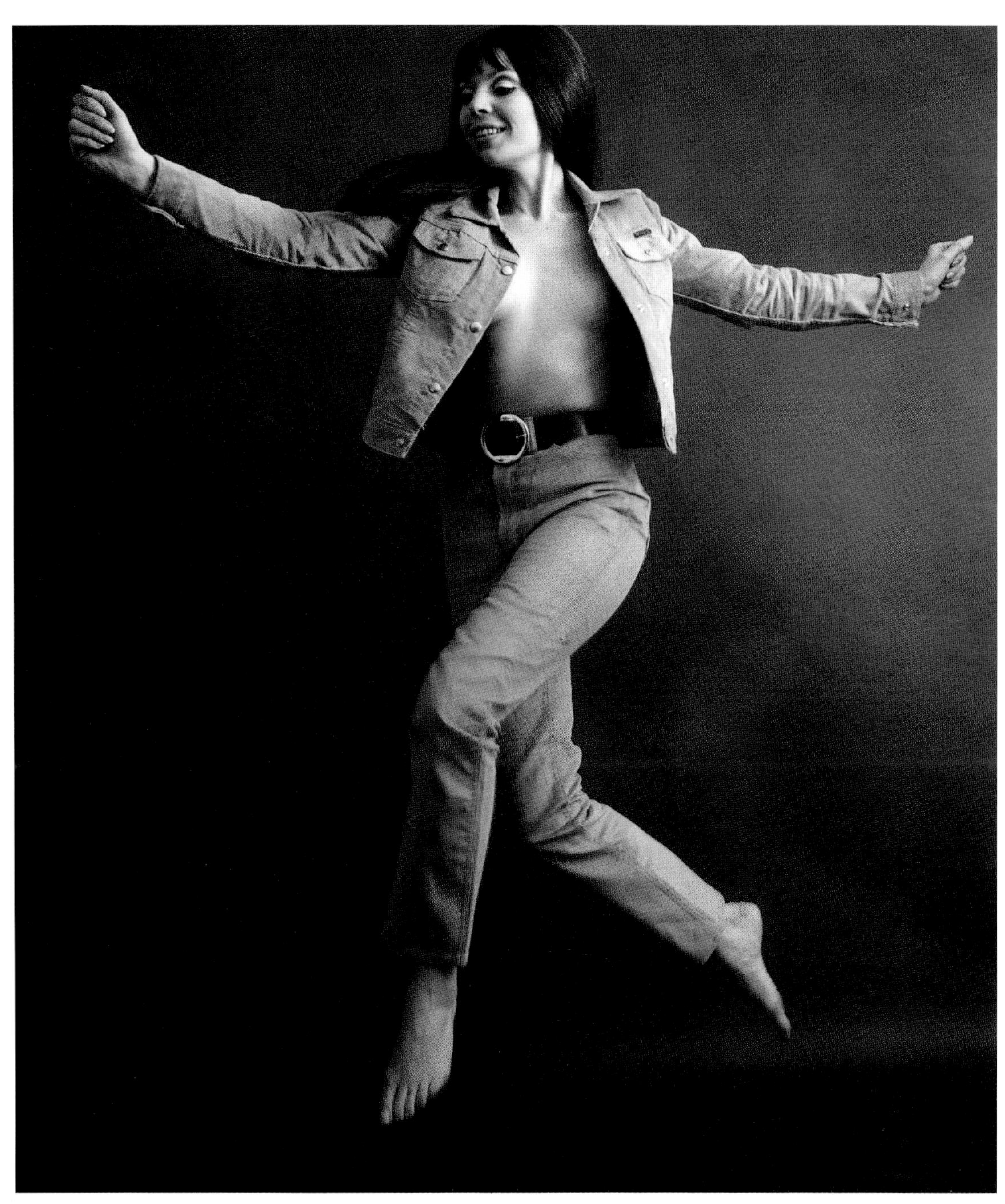

Eve Anthony, 1960s (no. 82)

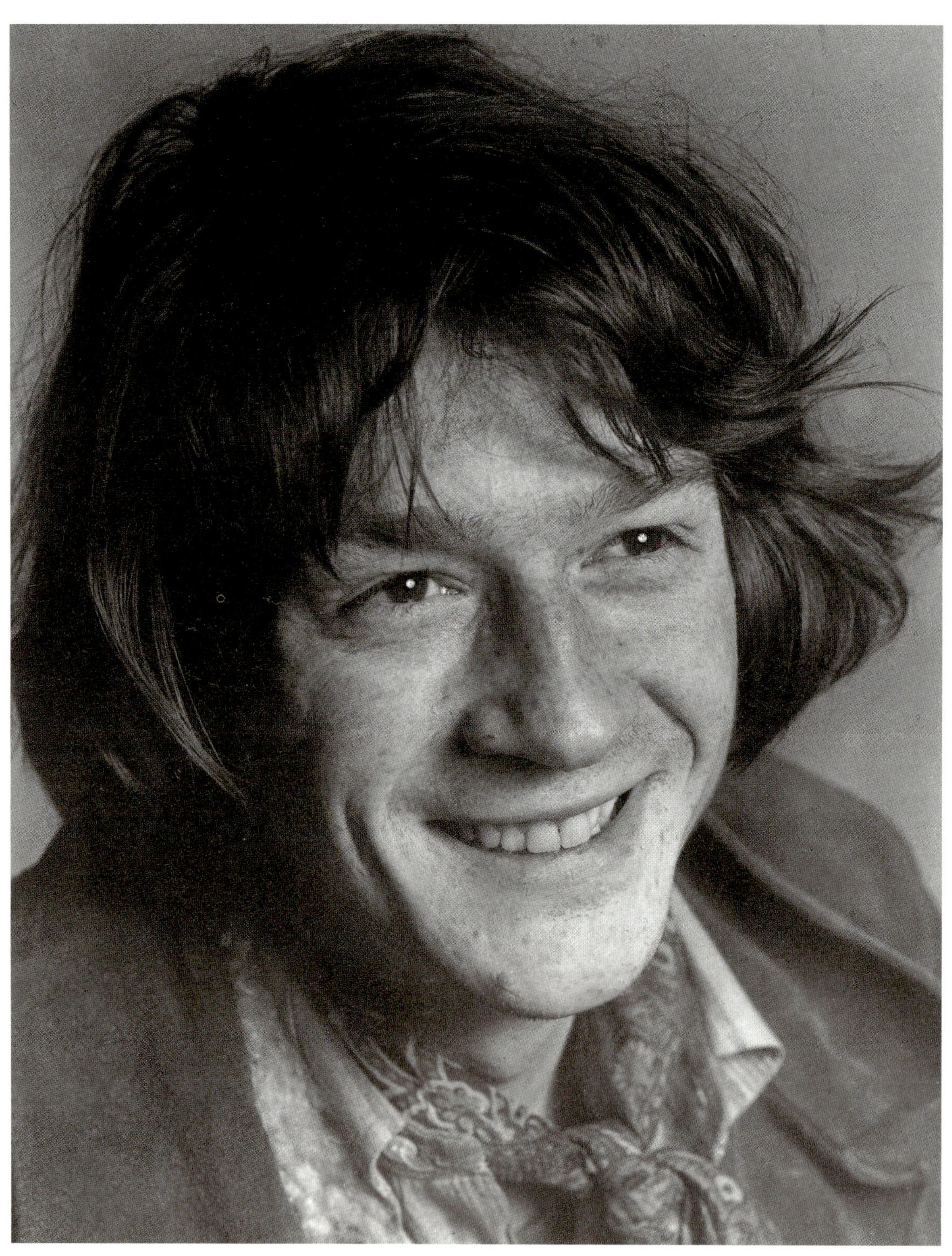

John Hurt, 1967 (no. 31)

Dizzy and **Yvonne**, 1967 (no. 78)

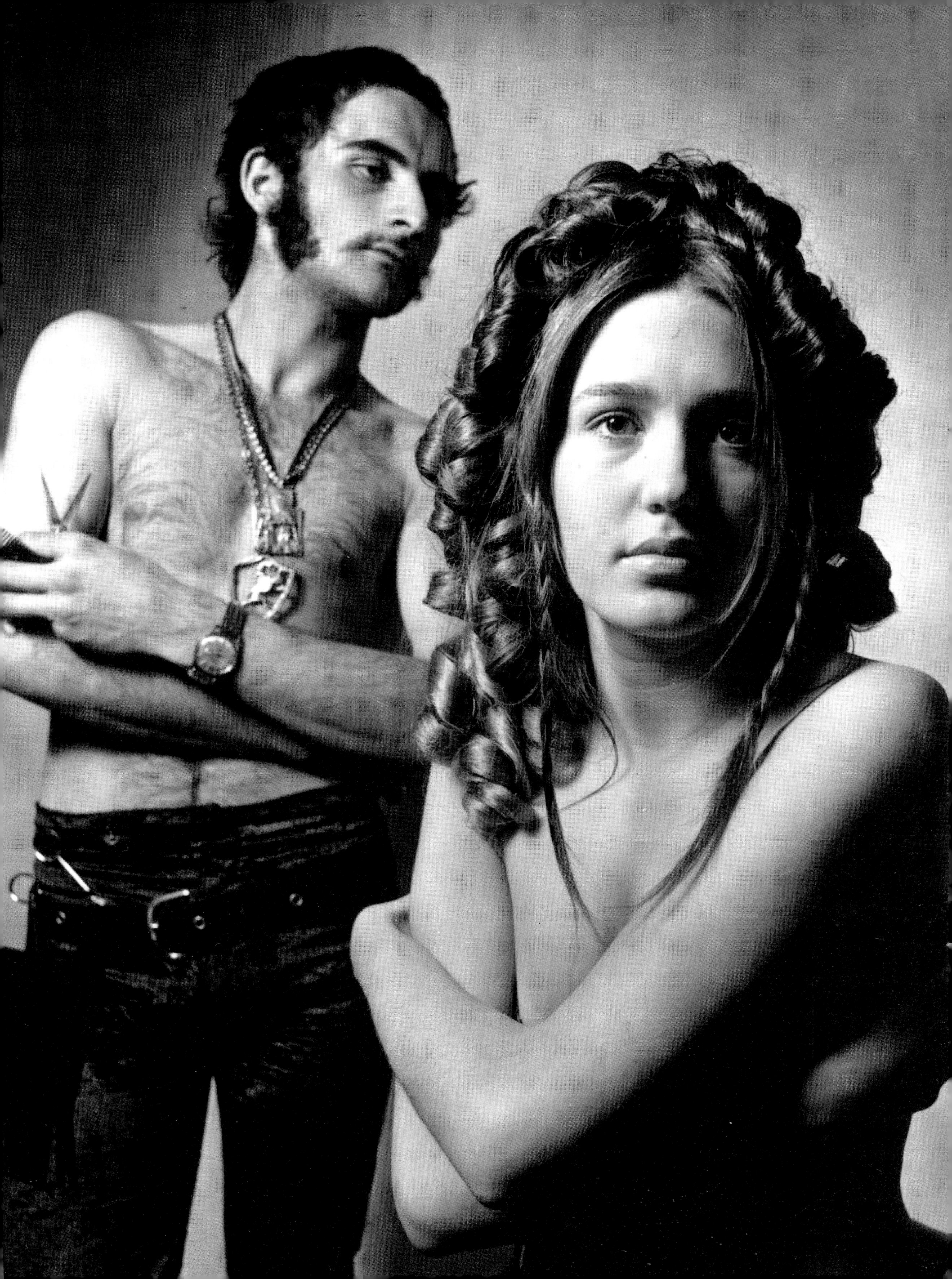

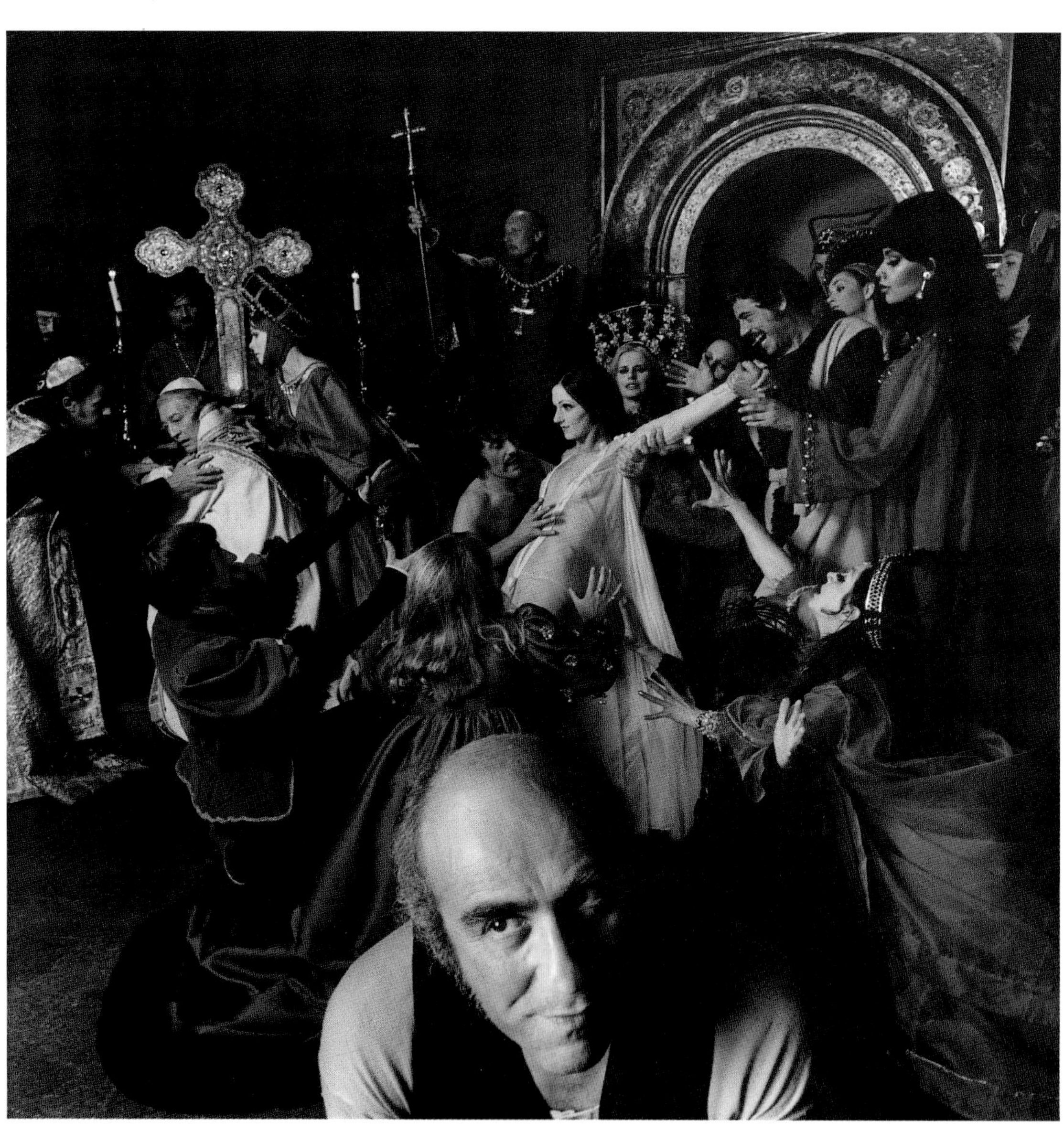

Warren Mitchell and the cast in *The Council of Love* (no. 76)

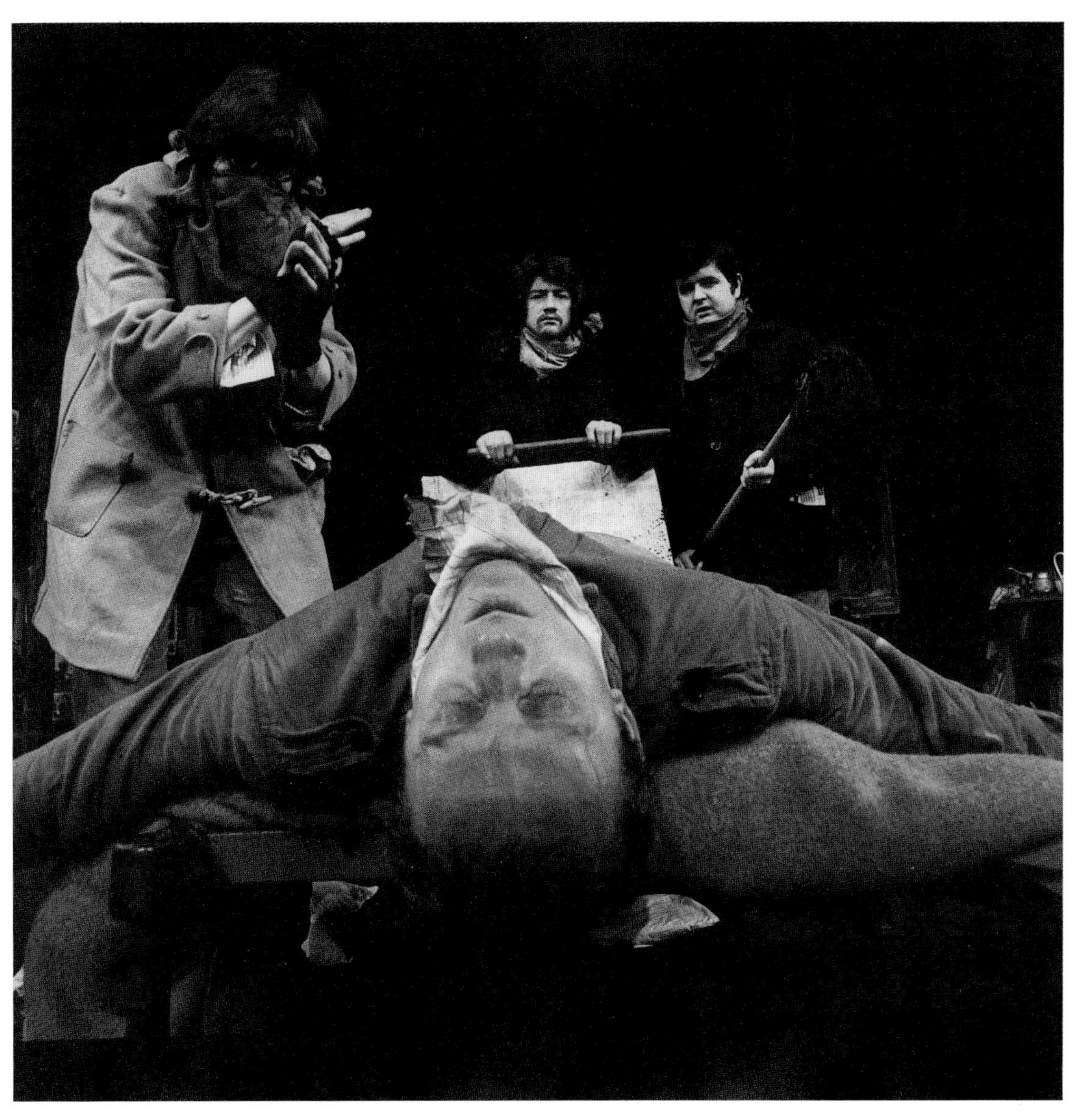

Rodney Bewes, **Tim Preece**, **John Hurt** and **Kenneth Colley** in *Little Malcolm and His Struggle Against the Eunuchs*, 1966 (no. 77)

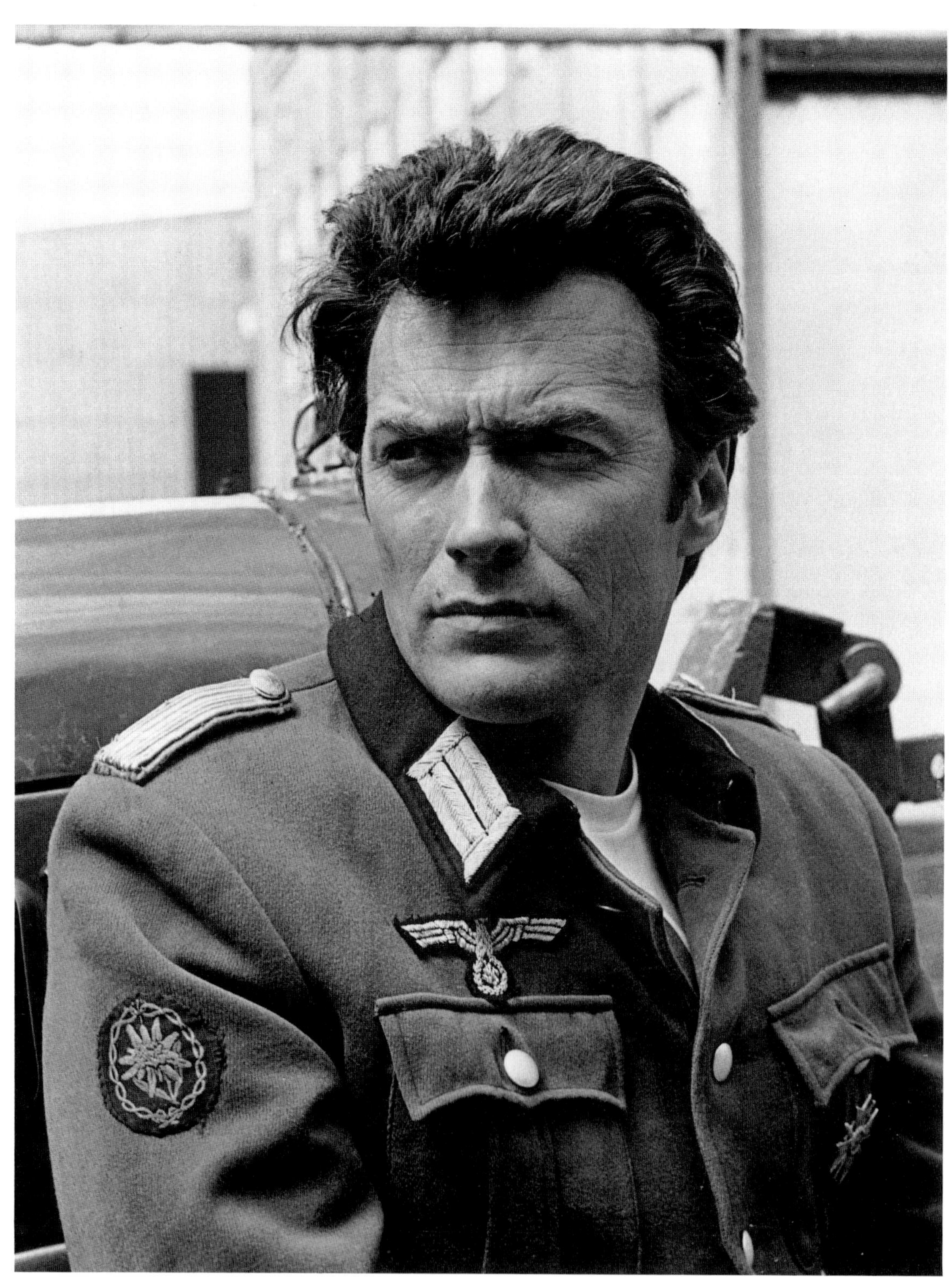

Clint Eastwood, 1969 (no. 85)

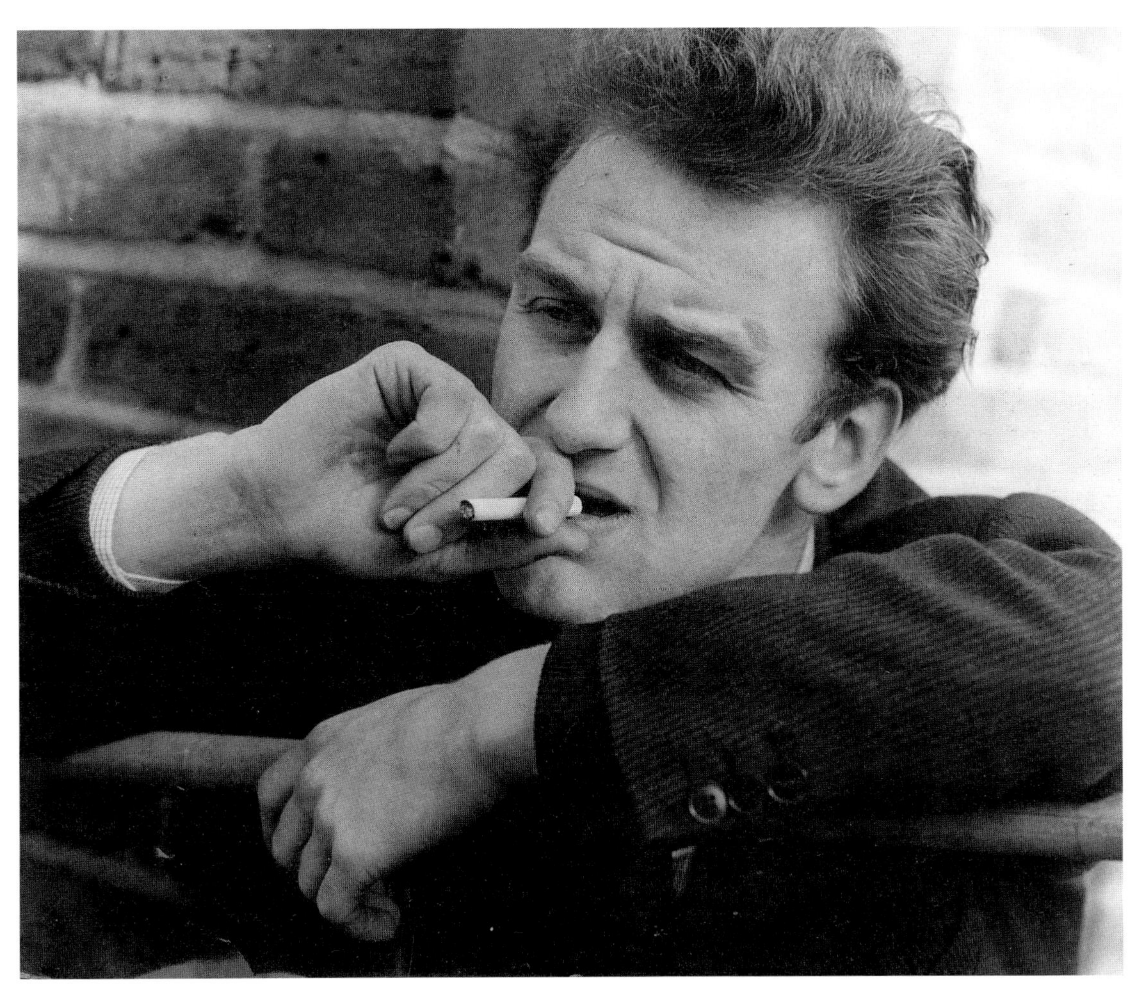

John Thaw, 1962 (no. 86)

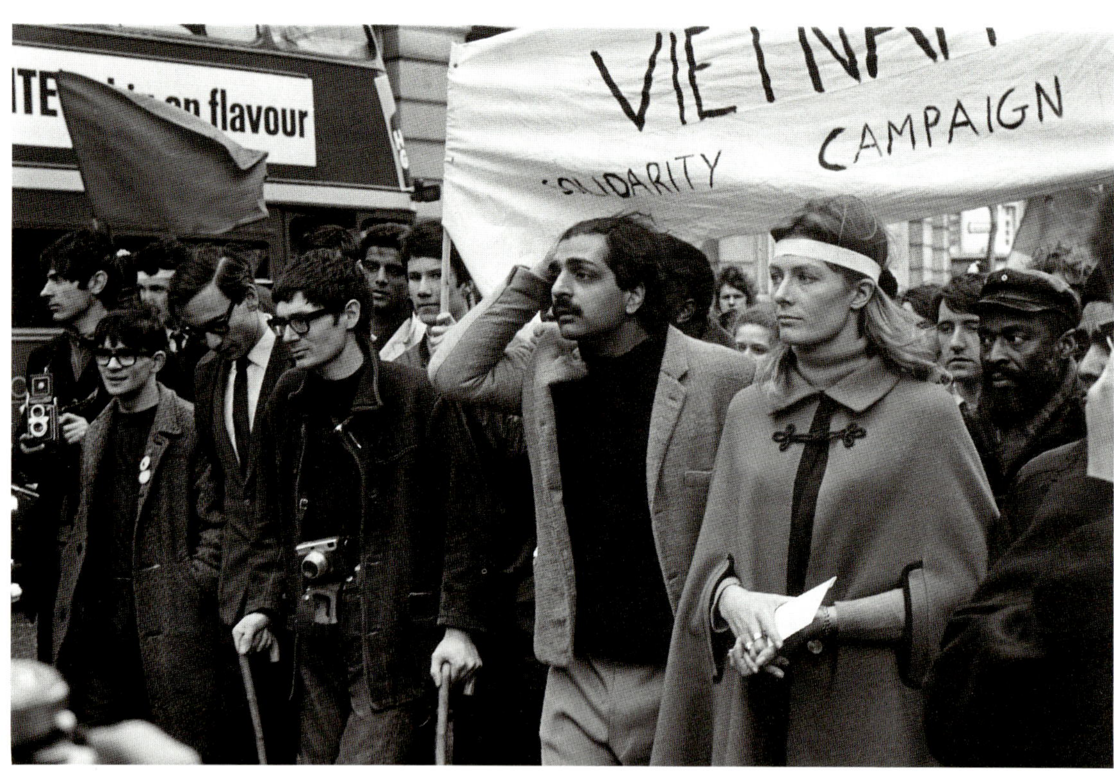

Tariq Ali and **Vanessa Redgrave** at anti-Vietnam War demonstration, London, 1968 (no. 87)

John Wells, 1965 (no. 66)

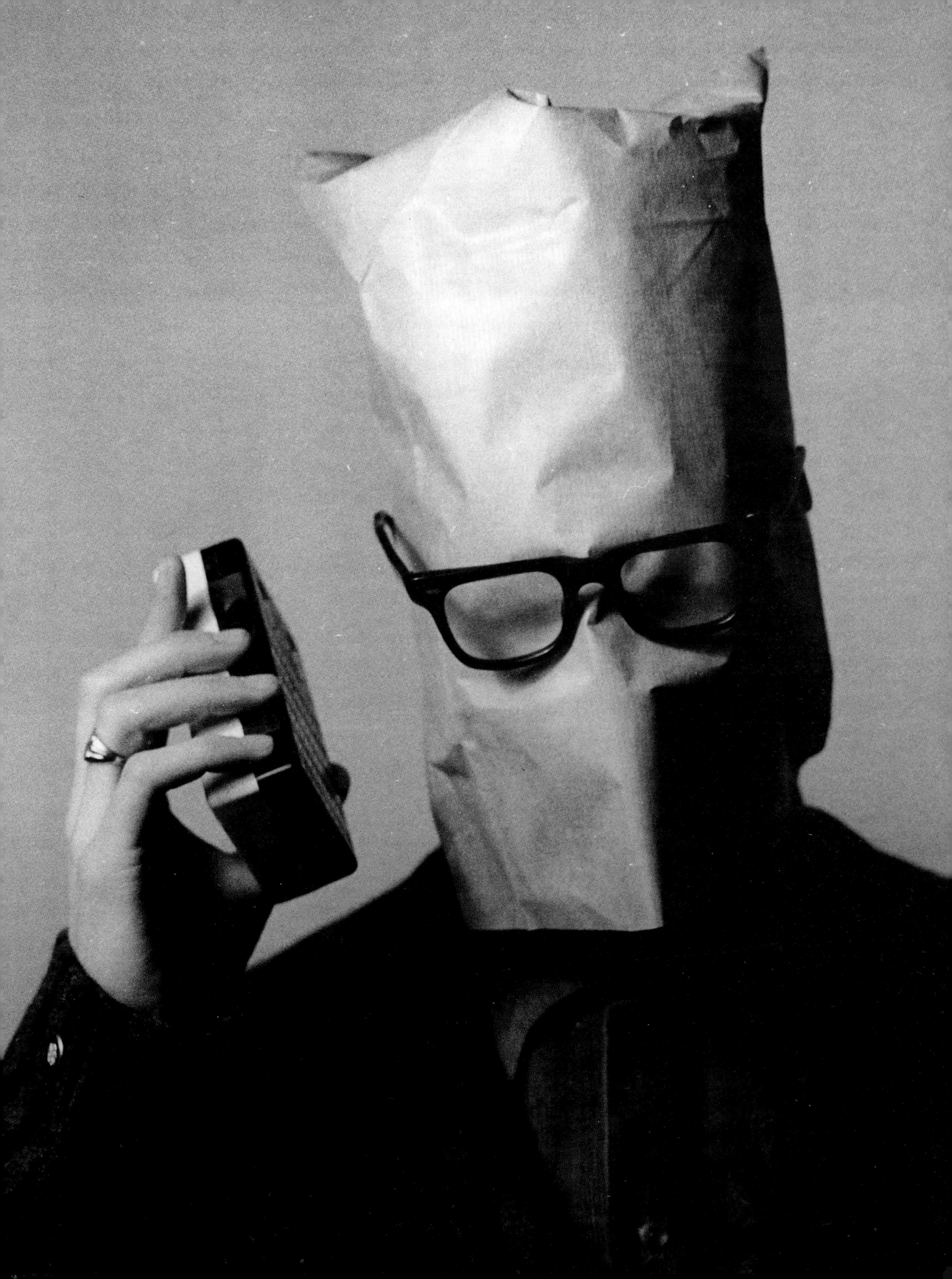

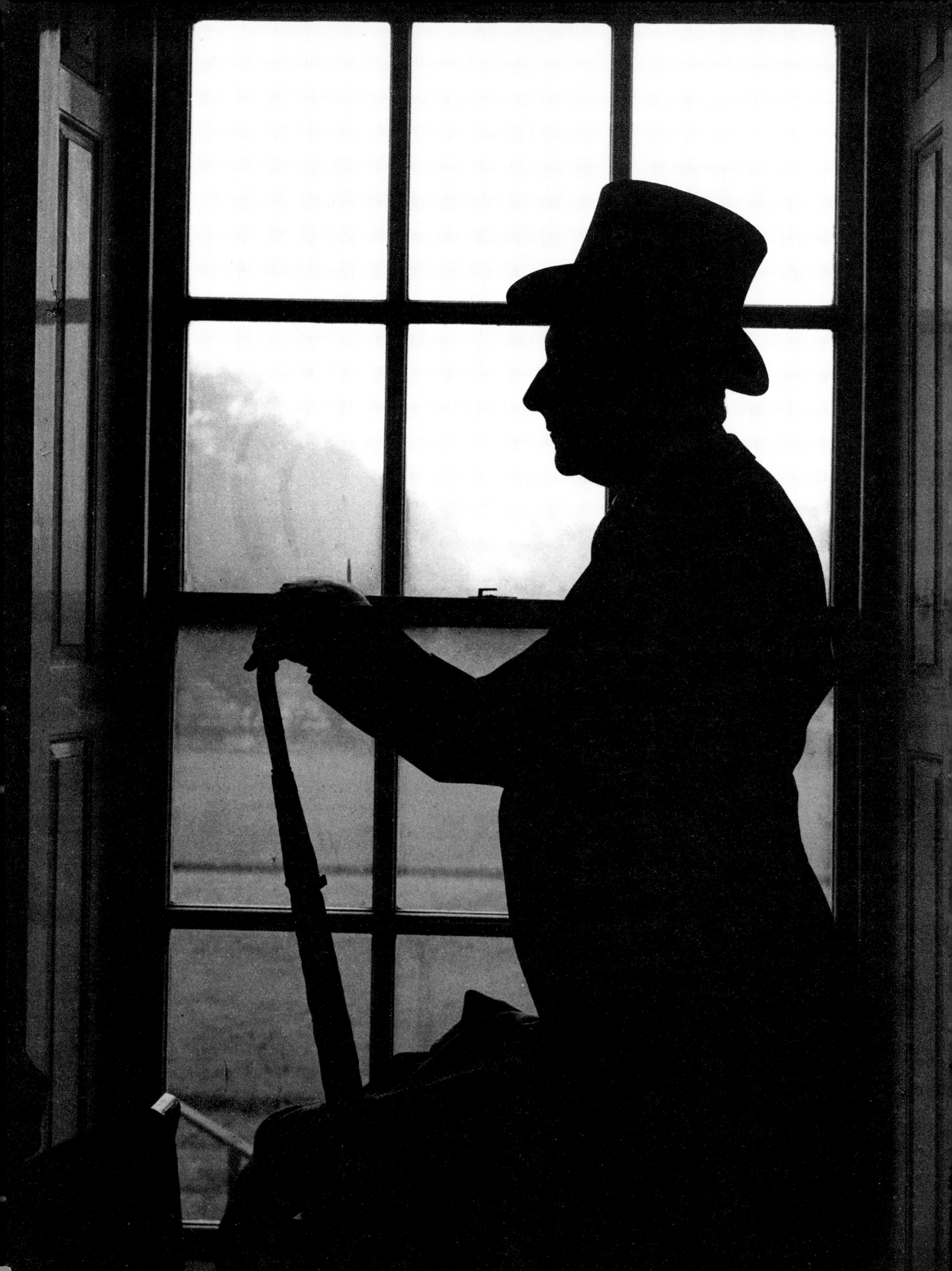

1 **Self-portrait** in a mirror with his wife **Patricia**
Paris, 1959

2 **Self-portrait**
London, 1954

3 **Bride in the Rain**
Hammersmith, 1957

4 **Watching the Trooping of the Colour**
London, 1957

5 **Trainspotter**
London, 1957

6 **Open Air Sculpture Exhibition**, Holland Park, London
The photograph shows Henry Moore's *Warrior and Shield*, 1953-4
1957

7 **Professor Albert Richardson's dog**
Published in *Tatler*, 15 November 1961

8 **Joan Wyndham**
Novelist
With her daughter, **Camilla**
Redcliffe Gardens
1955

9 **Terry Hamaton**
Graphic designer
1 Lansdowne Walk, Holland Park, London, 1960

10 **Sir Cecil Beaton** 1904-80
Photographer and stage designer
Informal portrait at a wedding reception
1960

11 **Raymond Loewy** 1893-1986
French-born American industrial designer
Photographed in his home in the South of France for *Tatler*, 1961

12 **Ken Coutts-Smith** born 1929
Painter and writer on art
Photographed on his barge in Chelsea, early 1960s

13 **Geoffrey Fisher, Archbishop of Canterbury** 1887-1972
Photographed at Canterbury for *Tatler*, 1960

14 **Jacqueline du Pré** 1945-87
Cellist
In the garden of her parents' home at Oxford, early 1960s

15 **Raymond Leppard**
born 1927
Conductor and composer
Photographed in his rooms at Cambridge for *Tatler*, 1960

16 **Sir Osbert Lancaster 1906-86**
Cartoonist and writer
Photographed on the roof of the *Daily Express* building
1960s

17 **Sir Peter** (Reginald Frederick) **Hall** born 1930
Theatre director
With his first wife, **Leslie Caron** born 1931
Actress
Photographed at home for a feature on Montpelier Square, London for *Tatler*, 1961

18 (Alan) **George** (Heywood) **Melly** born 1926
Professional blues singer
Early 1960s

19 **George Mann MacBeth**
born 1932
Writer and poet
Taken for the *Domesday* show at the Establishment Club
Early 1960s

20 **Lindsay Anderson**
born 1923
Film-maker and theatre director
Photographed for *Billy Liar* programme, 1960

21 **Keith Waterhouse** and **Willis Hall** (both born 1929)
Co-writers of *Billy Liar*, produced at the Cambridge Theatre, September 1960

22 **Tom Courtenay** born 1937
Actor and first replacement for stage role of *Billy Liar* and star of 1963 film
1961

23 **Albert Finney** born 1936
Stage and film actor
As Billy Fisher in *Billy Liar*, photographed outside the Cambridge Theatre, London, 1960

24 **Robin Ray** with his wife **Susan Stranks**
Television personalities
1960s

25 **Anthony Powell** born 1905
Novelist and author of *Afternoon Men* (1931)
With **Riccardo Arragno**, who adapted Powell's novel for stage; it was performed at the New Arts Theatre Club, London
1963

Cecil Beaton, 1960 (no. 10)

26 **Johnny Speight** born 1920
Writer for television
Publicity photograph for production of his play *Knacker's Yard* performed at the Arts Theatre Club, London, 16 January 1962

27 **Michael Caine** (Maurice Micklewhite) born 1933
Stage and film actor
Photographed on stage at the New Arts Theatre, London, in Peter Saunders' play *Next Time I'll Sing To You,* before leaving to film *Zulu,* January 1963

28 **Dame Judi Dench** born 1934
Television, theatre and film actress
Photographed on the film set for Anthony Simmons' film *Four In The Morning*, 1965

29 **Peter O'Toole** born 1932
Actor
Photographed at the Old Vic, London, in the title role of Brecht's first play, *Baal*, 1963

30 **John Antrobus** born 1933
Playwright; co-author with Spike Milligan of *The Bed-Sitting Room*
1960s

31 **John Hurt** born 1940
Actor
1967

32 **Sean Kenny** 1932-73
Stage designer
Photographed at work on his Las Vegas project, for *Scene* magazine, 1963

33 **James Wedge** born 1939
Hat designer and fashion photographer
Early 1960s

34 **Nancy Spain** 1917-64
Journalist, broadcaster and author
Early 1960s

35 **Edina Ronay**
Fashion model, later fashion designer
1963

36 **Susannah York** (Susannah Yolande Fletcher) born 1941
Actress
With her husband **Michael Wells**
Paris, 1961

37 **Jean Shrimpton** born 1942
Model
With **Chris Powell**
Model
Racecourse fashion feature for *Go!* (Shrimpton's first modelling assignment)
1961

38 **Twiggy** (Lesley Hornby) born 1949
With her manager **Justin de Villeneuve** (Nigel John Davies) born 1940
Street fashion feature for *London Life,* January 1966

39 **Charlotte Rampling** born 1945
Fashion model and actress
At her flat, London, 1963

40 **Tom Jones** (Thomas Jones Woodward) born 1940
Singer
Photographed during a costume fitting with Sylvia Gosse, early 1960s

41 **Adam Faith** (Terence Nelhams) born 1940
Pop singer and actor
Photographed with one of his Rolls-Royces for a magazine feature on eligible bachelors for *Woman's Day,* early 1960s

42 **Jim Dale** (as Vince Philpot) born 1935
Singer and actor
With **The Drags**
1960s

43 **Brian Epstein** 1934-67
Pop impresario
Liverpool, 1963

44 **Billy J. Kramer** (William Ashton) born 1943 and **Heinz**
Fashion feature for *She,* 1964

45 **The Small Faces: Steve Marriott** born 1947, **Ronnie 'Plonk' Lane** born 1946, **Jimmy Winston** born 1945 and **Kenny Jones** born 1948
Photograph commissioned by their manager Simon Napier-Bell, 1965

46 **Kenny Everett** born 1944
Disc jockey and television personality
With his wife **Lee** and pets
1960s

47 **Dave Clark** born 1942
Leader of the Dave Clark Five
Fashion feature for *She*, 1964

48 **Pauline Boty** 1938-66
Pop artist and actress
With a collection of paintings including *Scandal '63* for her exhibition held in September 1963

49 **Roddy Maude Roxby**
born 1930
Performer and actor
Photographed in Soho Square, London, for a revue at the Arts Theatre, *Three at Nine,* with Annie Ross, 1960s

50 **Sir Eduardo Paolozzi**
born 1924
Sculptor and printmaker
Photographed taking a class at the Royal College of Art, London, 1959

51 **Anthony Fry** born 1927
Painter
With **Sheila Scott-James** and their son **Wild**
(after Benvenuto Cellini's salt-cellar)
1964

52 **Sir Peter Maxwell Davies**
born 1934
Composer
Portrait taken at his home, commissioned by his agent James Murdoch, who also represented Harrison Birtwhistle (no. 53) with whom Maxwell Davies directed *The Pierrot Players,* 1967-70

53 **Harrison Birtwhistle**
born 1934
Composer
1960s

54 **Jeff Beck** born 1944
Singer
With his Afghan hound
Photograph taken for a portrait session, after leaving The Yardbirds for a solo career, 1967

55 **Donovan** (Donovan Phillips Leitch) born 1946
Singer-songwriter
1965

56 **Sian Phillips** and **Alan Badel**
Actors
With **Philip Wiseman**
Director
Rehearsal photograph for production of George Bernard Shaw's *Man and Superman* at the New Arts Theatre, November 1965

57 **Athol Fugard** born 1932
Playwright
With **Zaikes Mokae, John Berry** (director) and **Ian Bannen** born 1928
Rehearsal study for Fugard's *The Blood Knot* at the New Arts Theatre, London, taken for *Scene*, 1963

58 **Felicity Kendall** born 1946
Actress
With her first husband, **Drewe Henley** born 1941
Actor
1968

59 **John Cleese** born 1939 and **Connie Booth**
Writers and comedians
1968

60 **The Premise: Theodore J. Flicker, Joan Darling, James Frawley** and **Thomas Aldredge**
This revue was produced by William Donaldson at the Comedy Theatre, London
26 July 1962

61 Cast of **Beyond The Fringe: Jonathan Miller** (born 1934), **Peter Cook** (born 1937), **Dudley Moore** (born 1935) and **Alan Bennett** (born 1934)
Photographed at Brighton for front-of-house photographs for London production at Fortune Theatre, 1961

62 **Beyond The Fringe: Peter Cook** and **Dudley Moore**
Brighton promenade, 1961

63 **Beyond The Fringe: Alan Bennett, Peter Cook, Dudley Moore** and **Jonathan Miller**
Brighton, 1961

64 **Beyond The Fringe** cast on stage in spoof Shakespeare sketch, 1961

65 **Barry Humphries** born 1934
Actor and writer who first came to prominence with his one-man show at the Establishment Club
Photographed in his Little Venice flat with his Charles Conder fan designs
1962

66 **John Wells** born 1936
Posed as 'Spotty Muldoon' for *Private Eye* advice column, May 1965

67 **Eleanor Bron**
Actress and writer
1963

68 **Bernard Levin** born 1928
Journalist, author and critic
1963

69 **Bernard Levin**
1963

70 **Millicent Martin** born 1934
Resident singer on BBC Television's *That Was The Week That Was,* 1963

71 **David** (Paradine) **Frost** born 1930
Television interviewer and presenter
1963

72 **Private Eye** group 'Some of the Young Pacey People who make London Swing'
Left to right; back row: **Richard Ingrams, Tony Rushton, Paul Foot, Barry Fantoni, Jill Brooke**; middle row: **Gabby Hughes, Peter Usborne, unknown, Jan Elson, Michael Wale**; foreground: **John Wells**
1965

73 **Richard Ingrams** and **Tony Rushton** in *Private Eye* offices for a Swiss fashion advertisement. 1966

74 **Barry Fantoni** as 'Larry Flies'
Spoof feature based on Lord Snowdon's book on British artists, *Private View*
Published in *Private Eye,*
12 November 1965

75 **Private Eye Fashion:** 'The Loony Look' posed by **Barry Fantoni, Diana Clarke** and **Willie Rushton**
Published 31 March 1967

76 **The Council of Love: Warren Mitchell** (Satan), **Imogen Claire** (Lucretia Borgia; centre) and the cast, performed at the Criterion Theatre, 1970

77 **Little Malcolm and His Struggle Against the Eunuchs**: Four of the cast of David Halliwell's play: **Rodney Bewes, Tim Preece, John Hurt** and **Kenneth Colley** 1966

78 **Dizzy**
Hairdresser
With **Yvonne**, his girlfriend model
Studio portait taken for his Carnaby Street salon, 1967

79 **Chain-mail Fashion**
Stylists prepare a model for a chain-mail fashion feature for *She*
1969

80 **Chain-mail Fashion**
Published in November 1969 issue of *She*

81 **Mynah Bird**
Fashion model
With **Peter Smith**
Fashion photographer
On Camber Sands
1960s

82 **Eve Anthony**
Fashion model
Advertising photograph for Lee Cooper jeans
11960s

83 **Tinka Patterson**
Artist and male fashion model
1960s

84 **Flick Colby**
Modern dance choreographer
1960s

85 **Clint Eastwood** born 1930
Actor and director
Photographed off-set during filming of *Where Eagles Dare*, Elstree Studio, 1969

86 **John Thaw** born 1942
Television and film actor
Soho, London, 1962

87 **Anti-Vietnam War demonstration**, Grosvenor Square, London
The demonstration was led by **Tariq Ali** born 1943 and **Vanessa Redgrave** born 1937
27 October 1968

88 **Sir John Betjeman** 1906-84
Poet Laureate
Photographed for *Private Eye's* architecture column 'Nooks and Corners' as one in a series on eyesores of London
1970

89 **Christine Keeler** born 1942
Publicity photographs for a proposed film of her life which was never made
1963

90 **Christine Keeler**
Three contact sheets
1963

91 **Joe Orton** 1933-67
Playwright
Commissioned for the American production of *Entertaining Mr Sloane*, 1965

92 **Joe Orton**
1965

93 **Joe Orton**
Three contact sheets
1965

Index of subjects illustrated

All references are to page numbers

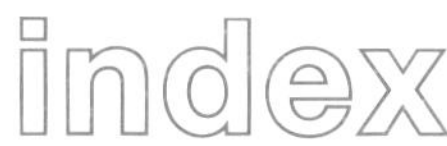